STAR DUST FALLING

THE STORY OF THE PLANE THAT VANISHED

JAY RAYNER

Doubleday

LONDON · NEW YORK · TORONTO · SYDNEY · AUCKLAND

TRANSWORLD PUBLISHERS
61–63 Uxbridge Road, London W5 5SA
a division of The Random House Group Ltd

RANDOM HOUSE AUSTRALIA (PTY) LTD
20 Alfred Street, Milsons Point, Sydney,
New South Wales 2061, Australia

RANDOM HOUSE NEW ZEALAND LTD
18 Poland Road, Glenfield, Auckland 10, New Zealand

RANDOM HOUSE SOUTH AFRICA (PTY) LTD
Endulini, 5a Jubilee Road, Parktown 2193, South Africa

Published 2002 by Doubleday
a division of Transworld Publishers

A catalogue record for this book is available from the British Library.
ISBN 0385 60226X

Typeset in 10/16pt Sabon by Falcon Oast Graphic Art Ltd.

Printed in Great Britain
by Mackays of Chatham plc, Chatham, Kent

1 3 5 7 9 10 8 6 4 2

For Eddie:
a big adventure for a little boy
at the beginning of his own

Author's Note
Apart from those rare occasions
clearly indicated in the text as
speculation, all direct speech or internal
monologue is based on interviews with
those involved or those who knew them
or documents about them.
None is 'imagined'.

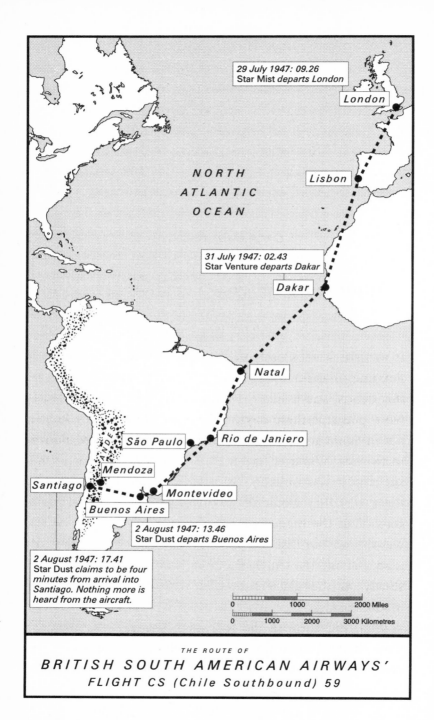

29 July 1947: 09.26
Star Mist *departs London*

London

NORTH

ATLANTIC

OCEAN

Lisbon

31 July 1947: 02.43
Star Venture *departs Dakar*

Dakar

Natal

São Paulo   *Rio de Janiero*

Mendoza

Santiago

Montevideo

Buenos Aires

2 August 1947: 13.46
Star Dust *departs Buenos Aires*

2 August 1947: 17.41
Star Dust *claims to be four*
minutes from arrival into
Santiago. Nothing more is
heard from the aircraft.

| 0 | | 1000 | | 2000 Miles |
| 0 | 1000 | 2000 | | 3000 Kilometres |

THE ROUTE OF

BRITISH SOUTH AMERICAN AIRWAYS'
FLIGHT CS (Chile Southbound) 59

CHAPTER ONE

Tupungato, High Andes, Argentina

January 1998

IT WAS THE SHREDS OF PINSTRIPE MATERIAL, HELD FAST IN THE moraine, that finally brought it home to them: whatever this debris was it had not arrived here recently. Nobody wore pinstripe these days, or at least nobody they knew; not in Santiago to the west of the mountains or Mendoza to the east. Whoever had worn it had done so a long time ago and it was unlikely, looking at the wreckage around them, that they would be in any position to claim owner- ship. That the ragged pieces of cloth had survived intact was of little surprise. Up here, above 4,500 metres, the air is so thin and the temperatures so low that decay moves as slowly as the glaciers that etch their way across the mountainsides.

What did surprise the two men was that they should have chanced upon the wreckage like this, after so many years. Because whatever else Pablo Reguera and Fernando

Garmendia were doing up here they were certainly not on the hunt for ancient plane wrecks. As the 23-year-old climbers from Tandil in Buenos Aires province would readily have told anybody who asked, this expedition was something special: it was a journey in the footsteps of dead men, an attempt to pay tribute, and they neither sought nor craved diversion. Thirteen years earlier Guillermo Vierio, one of Argentina's greatest Andean mountaineers – or *andinistas* – had attempted this very same climb. Accompanied by his student, Jorge Rabal, Vierio set out from Tandil determined to conquer the virgin south-eastern route of Tupungato, an extinct volcano. The two men told the soldiers manning the lonely army station at the mouth of the valley below that they would be back by 1 February. When they had not returned by Valentine's Day the army mounted a rescue attempt on foot and by mule, but the soldiers were beaten back by the vicious weather that can close in so quickly in the high Andes, even during the summer months of January and February. A few days later, when the skies cleared, they launched a second attempt, this time using a Lama helicopter. It was a risky exercise. At these altitudes a sudden downdraught can leave the Lama under-powered and spiralling towards the rocky ground. But they were fortunate with the winds and were able to bring the helicopter in to land at a site 4,500 metres up the mountain. After that the soldiers' luck ran out: close to the ragged edge of a glacier, they found the bodies of Vierio and Rabal.

As children Reguera and Garmendia had known and admired both men, particularly Vierio. His death affected them greatly. He was a hero to them, in a small town where heroes were in short supply. He was the one who went out and did the things they were only allowed to dream about. They listened to his stories and, after his death, decided that one day they would complete the climb that had killed him. In 1995, on the tenth anniversary, they made their first attempt. They carried a brass plaque recording the names of both men and how they had died, which they were to leave at the summit. The plaque returned with them to Tandil. Like so many others they were defeated by the weather.

Three years later, they were trying again. Once more it looked like they were destined to fail. There was no shame in that. At 6,800 metres Tupungato may not be the highest mountain in the Americas – that honour is held by the nearby Aconcagua at 6,959 metres – but it is the most challenging. For all the lyricism in its name Aconcagua is dismissed by many experienced climbers as little more than a stiff walk. Tupungato, on the other hand, is a serious piece of rock and ice. On Tupungato winds regularly reach ninety miles an hour, even in the summer, as air plunges down hard over the summit. When those winds pick up the snow and ice from the upper reaches they blow a blinding white that smothers anything foolish enough to stand in their path. Temperatures drop swiftly to 40 or 50 degrees below zero. Like Aconcagua, it was first conquered in 1897, but since then only half a dozen people a year have made it to the top and far too many have died trying. Part of the challenge lies in its location. Tupungato sits in an isolated valley close to the border with Chile. Just getting to its base requires an exhausting hike up and over the harsh ridges of a mountain called El Fraile, the Priest. Religious imagery is rife in this region of the Andes, where death comes too easily. If you make it over the Priest's backbone and up the first 4,000 metres or so of Tupungato itself, you have to contend with *los penitentes*, brutal towers of spiked ice two or three metres tall that cluster about the summit and which were named for their resemblance to pious, forbidding monks, their heads bowed low beneath sharply peaked cowls. If a god exists at all in these parts it is a thoroughly vengeful one.

Reguera and Garmendia first approached the summit by following a mountain river but the *penitentes*, ever bigger and ever closer together the higher up they went, conspired to block their way. Angry and despondent, they turned back, taking a shortcut down the glacier in the hope that they might be able to find another route to the top. This time they were determined not to take the plaque home with them. Unknowingly they made camp close to where Vierio's and Rabal's bodies had been recovered, at the fractured edge of the glacier. The next morning they set off again, Reguera leading, Garmendia behind.

They had been walking for only a few minutes when Garmendia called ahead to Reguera and drew his attention to an engine on the ice. Reguera stopped and took off the sunglasses that he always wore against the sharp mountain glare when he was climbing. On the ground next to him, resting on a pedestal of ice, was a chunk of what did indeed look like an engine, if a small one. Inscribed on the side were the words '–OLLS ROYCE', the first letter of the first word apparently torn away.

Reguera laughed. 'How did they get a car up here?' he said.

It was exactly the kind of poor joke Garmendia expected of his companion. Evidently it belonged to an aircraft although they had no idea which one; the Andes are as famous for swallowing up aviators as they are for killing mountaineers. The very first airman to cross them, an Argentinian called Benjamin Matienzo, who piloted his Morone Monoplane between the peaks on 13 April 1918, was also the very first to be lost here, during a trip the following year. It took them months to locate his body and when they found it, lying grotesquely twisted on the bare earth hard by a pass called La Casa de los Mines, it was well preserved by the conditions at high altitude. Of his plane, a Newport, there was no sign. That wasn't found for another thirty-one years, when it was discovered miles away just over the border in Chile by a team of meteorologists. They brought it down and took it to the Argentinian air force museum, *Museo Nacional de Aeronautica*, in Buenos Aires. The crumpled wreck was put on display in a big glass and oak box guarded by fine carvings of eagles. Since that crash dozens of aircraft have been lost to the crags and passes. While nobody has officially set out to count them, one amateur historian has identified sixty-six on the Argentinian side of the border since Matienzo apparently fell to his death. The most recent is a Lama helicopter which crashed in 1996.

Reguera and Garmendia were more interested in climbing mountains than in the fate of aircraft lost among them. Still, wreckage at 4,500 metres was worth a little of their time. They began to scan the rocky landscape surrounding the lump of engine. Nearby they found pieces of fuselage. There were wing sections, the metal bleached white by the sun and wind, and parts of the plane's electrical wiring system. Soon they were coming across fragments of clothing, including those strips of heavy pinstripe material. They took no photographs and didn't even bother to record the location. In his notebook, under the heading '26 January 1998', Garmendia wrote simply, 'We found a Rolls Roice engine,' taking so little time over the sentence that he failed to get the correct spelling of the British manu-facturer's name.

They didn't for a moment think they had solved one of the greatest aviation mysteries of all time. The find was a mere curio on the way to greater achievements. They had other things to do. They had a mountain to climb.

CHAPTER TWO

Over Alexander Bay, Southern Africa

October 1938

FROM THE AIR ALEXANDER BAY AT THE MOUTH OF THE ORANGE river boasted one important quality as far as Don Bennett was concerned: it was somewhere to land. Granted, there was no dedicated seaplane station down there, and the yellow sands of the desert hardly made for a handsome landscape as they slipped away feebly into the dun-coloured waters below, but there was at least a settlement on one riverbank with what looked like an aerodrome nearby. They could get hold of fuel there. In any case, there was no choice. The handpump they had taken to using many hours before when the electric pumps failed was now sucking only air from the converted fuel tanks in the floats. If they didn't put down now gravity would do the job for them and Bennett wasn't having that. He might not be landing where he would have liked. It might not promise the reception he had long dreamed of. But he was still about to win himself a serious place in aviation history. He was damned if this landing was going to be anything other than textbook.

Bennett, just twenty-eight years old, was hungry for success. Get it right, bring them down on to the river safely, and he would never again need to explain within aviation circles who he was. The serious young man from Queensland, Australia, had a high opinion of himself – though only with justification, he would say. His peers would later refer to him as the master airman. He was the one who understood instinctively what it took to be up there, plotting a course through the quixotic eddies and sudden wind shear in the days before jet thrust or global positioning. Bennett would hungrily accept the accolade even though he had no idea where this extraordinary facility came from.

Donald Clifford Tyndall Bennett was born on his father's cattle station at Toowoomba in 1910. His was a stolid family of teetotallers and Methodists which sent its sons into the professions. Two of Bennett's three brothers were lawyers, the third a doctor, and the youngest boy was expected to do something equally respectable. He was not impressive at school, however, and his father decided he did not justify the expense of a costly university education. Instead he stayed on the ranch, playing the outback Australian until he realized that he had even less affinity for cattle or the deep red dust of Toowoomba than he did for school work. He needed something else. He needed a challenge. The wide, empty Queensland skies overhead gave it to him.

Later in life he would claim memories of a flying exhibition given in his home town by the Wright brothers when he could not have been much more than three years old. Whether he genuinely did remember the event, or merely appropriated the memory, the story at least gave him a kind of exquisite lineage; he was old enough to have witnessed the pioneers at work. The Wright brothers aside, there were other great aviation moments he definitely was old enough to recall. In 1928 he watched an Australian pilot called Bert Hinkler arrive near Toowoomba after a mammoth solo flight all the way from England; in 1930 he saw the great Amy Johnson crash-land in a cornfield during the closing stages of her journey to Australia, the first by a woman. Her plane toppled over as it came to a halt and ended up on its nose, but she emerged unharmed. The stoical kind of heroism in these dramas appealed to the young Don Bennett. It all made sense to him, much more so than the tight circumlocutions of the law or the biological complexities of medicine. In 1930, despite opposition from his family, Bennett joined the Royal Australian Air Force. They told him that on completing his training he would be posted to England to join the Royal Air Force. Bennett was delighted. His mother was born in England and his grandfather had been a doctor there who emigrated after a murky dispute with the British Medical Association. 'The only crime an Englishman cannot for-give,' the old man once said, 'is to be right.' Although his grandson would become a strident patriot for his adopted country, in the way of so many colonials who had been nurtured on its grand mythologies, this was a slogan that would stay with him. It reinforced every one of his prejudices against a certain kind of Englishman, the plodding chap who, he said, placed rules and regulations before the skills offered by experience.

In short, Bennett considered himself a man of action. Others could lecture and pontificate. Others could talk and blather. Bennett, businesslike and severe, would be the one to get on with the job. He did not drink and he did not smoke. He had little time for the frivolous and never mastered the point of social niceties or the emotional complexities of humour. His sharp, lightly chiselled features and sloping, hooded eyes, fixed permanently in a sceptical squint as though he were forever staring into the sun, did not ease the austere image. But, by God, the man could fly. In the RAF he developed a fearsome reputation both for mastering new aircraft and for navigating them. By 1935, when he left the service, he had flown twenty-one different types of plane and crashed only one of them (when, in quick succession, he ran out of fuel, into a cold front and finally into a field; like Amy Johnson's plane in Australia, it tipped over on to its nose. Bennett, forever charmed in matters of calamity, was uninjured). That same year he wrote *The Complete Air Navigator*, a book which would remain the key text on the subject for the next three decades. It was something of a bizarre wedding present for his Swiss-born wife, Ly. He wrote it during their honeymoon, on board a cruise ship to Australia and surrounded by passengers whom he accused of being 'violently and aggressively engaged in a waste of time'. Don Bennett did not hold with wasting time, not even on his honeymoon.

Early in 1936 he joined Imperial Airways, one of the first of the British long-haul carriers. It was already operating routes to South Africa and, with Qantas, to Australia. Mostly the airlines used seaplanes: vast flying boats that hopped their way across the world in stages of a few hundred miles at a time. Bennett was soon in command of his own Empire Flying Boat and, in 1937, he became the first pilot to complete the journey from Alexandria in Egypt to Southampton in the space of one day. It was regarded at the time as a serious achievement, but Bennett had his eyes set on bigger things.

Ever since John Alcock and Arthur Whitten Brown flew the Atlantic non-stop for the first time in June 1919 the race had been on to find a way to make hard cash out of the route. Carrying two people across the distance was all well and good but there was no profit in it. The problem – and it was one that would dog commercial aviation for decades – was weight. To complete great distances an aircraft would have to carry so much fuel that, on top of the burden of either passengers or cargo, it would be far too heavy to take off. The Germans were experimenting with great, taut-skinned airships but they were slow and unwieldy. The explosion of the *Hindenburg* in New Jersey in 1937 would eventually prove them unfashionably lethal as well. Another German team was working on a system to catapult seaplanes into the air. It worked, and was used by Lufthansa on a mail route to South America, but there were concerns over the strain caused by the chest-thumping acceleration the pilots were forced to endure. It was equivalent to four times gravity; paying passengers could not be forced to suffer that, even given the pioneering spirit of the age.

In Britain Imperial Airways was working on two solutions. The first was the in-flight refuelling of flying boats over the Atlantic from the isolated Azores, but that had failed to get off the drawing board. The other method was the brainchild of Major Robert Mayo, the quiet and unassuming technical manager of Imperial. With the help of the British manufacturers Short Bros, Mayo had come up with an ingenious solution: give the aircraft a piggyback ride into the air. The prototype they built cost £60,000, a hefty investment even with some of the cash coming from the British government. At least they got two planes for their money. At the bottom of Mayo's chunky, boy's-own invention was a large four-engined seaplane, eventually named the *Maia*, which would carry just enough fuel for take-off and return. A smaller four-engined seaplane – the *Mercury* – would be clipped on top. As they ascended the smaller, more heavily loaded *Mercury* would take on more and more of the lifting duties. When they had reached the right altitude, both pilots would pull the release catch at the same time and they would spring apart. The equipment would be cheaper than the catapult system and, Mayo argued, eminently more flexible. (Forty years later, when NASA was experimenting with releasing the prototype Space Shuttle from the top of a Boeing 747, the test crew put up a notice in the hangar. It read: 'Remember. The Brits did it first.')

Bennett adored the sound of the project. It was dashing, cutting-edge stuff; just the thing for a man of action. In

1938 he managed to get himself posted to the *Mercury–Maia* testing centre down at Felixstowe on the east coast, though he despaired at the length of time it took to get the research work done. 'Its laborious processes were unbelievable,' he announced later, as he so often would of so many other bureaucracies that infuriated him. 'I really think that if I had not been present during the whole of the tests the Felixstowe staff would have taken at least two years to complete them.' Finally in the summer of 1938 he managed to drag what had now become known as the Mayo Composite off its testing programme and into the real world. He obtained permission to attempt the Atlantic crossing despite grave doubts from within the British government's Air Ministry. They claimed the prototype had nowhere near the required range. It was his first experience of a particularly tiresome kind of civil servant who, as Bennett saw it, was only ever going to be an enemy of progress.

The Mayo Composite, he argued, could do the job. Let him prove it, he said. The ministry eventually agreed. On 20 July 1938 he and his radio operator took off carrying the first commercial load – mostly newspapers and movie reels – to cross from Europe to America by air. They arrived in Montreal 20 hours and 20 minutes later having covered almost 3,000 miles.

Bennett was sure he could do more. The moment he arrived back at Southampton he cornered the air minister, Sir Kingsley Wood, who had turned out as part of the welcoming committee. He had an idea. Why didn't he have a crack at the seaplane distance record? It then stood at

4,500 miles. Convert the *Mercury*'s floats to carry extra fuel and it could easily be done, he said. It had to be done. He proposed flying from Southampton to Cape Town, which would more than nail the record. The government sceptics, now the enthusiasts, suggested he went even further. Why not attempt the overall aviation distance record of more than 6,000 miles by taking off from Dundee? Bennett could hardly say no. Men of action did not turn their noses up at a challenge. He set the attempt for the autumn, although for weeks he and his team were grounded at Leuchars as the British prime minister, Neville Chamberlain, appeased Adolf Hitler's territorial ambitions. Eventually the prime minister returned waving his sheet of paper and talking up his peace deal of which Bennett, as if limbering up for the war to come, declared himself an arch opponent. The so-called peace deal, he said, could only ever be temporary but at least it presented the opportunity he needed: on 6 October 1938 Bennett and his co-pilot, Ian Harvey, took off in the Mayo Composite. The *Mercury* was carrying almost 50 per cent more than its normal maximum load in fuel.

From the start the trip was hazardous. Because of the extra weight the two aircraft had to separate at a much higher speed than had been attempted before. The stress ripped off part of an engine cowling, damaging the sleek aerodynamic profile of the *Mercury* and reducing its range – the overall distance the plane could travel – by up to four per cent. In the short term they had to burn extra fuel simply to keep themselves aloft. Over southern England they hit a cold front which forced them down to lower altitudes to avoid icing. Bennett knew they would later have to regain the height to clear the peaks of the Atlas mountains of North Africa. That, in turn, would need more fuel. For a while he even considered abandoning the attempt. Eventually he concluded there was little point. *Mercury* was too heavy to land carrying so much fuel and would stay that way for at least twenty-four hours. By that time they could be out over warm African thermals. They might as well continue, if only to see what first light would bring. For much of that first night, the only messages he sent back were heavy with gloom.

By sunrise, though, they were beneath clear skies flying over a Saharan desert of undulating dunes. Everything seemed set fair. Then the electric pumps gave out and they were forced to start shifting the 1,400 gallons stored in the floats the ten feet up to the wings by hand. They were now at 12,000 feet, where lungs fight for what meagre draught of oxygen there is, and it was gruelling, aching work. They could not be at all certain of completing it successfully. As the sun began to set over Nigeria on the second day Bennett was faced with another dilemma. There was nowhere below him he could land a seaplane during darkness if they did run out of fuel. He wouldn't even be sure whether he was over land or the safety of sea until he had all but touched down and by then it would be too late. Either he made for the coast now and brought her down at twilight without any certainty of getting her back up again, or he took the risk and decided to push on through the night. Not for the first or the last time in his career he took the risk, though as the hours of darkness slipped slowly by he began to wonder if he had made the right decision. Soon his co-pilot was hallucinating. 'Where is the other chap?' he asked of his captain. 'He's gone. I know he has gone.' Bennett had to reassure Harvey that it was the two of them up there in the low-lit gloom of an African night, desperately pumping fuel to keep them aloft. As he turned the crank in the early hours, gulping down air to get much-needed oxygen to his exhausted muscles, one thing became obvious. They were not going to make it to Cape Town. He needed to find somewhere to land. Alexander Bay finally came into view at dawn as the tanks showed empty. Bennett announced it would have to be their landing spot. He had no way of knowing that it was the heart of the South African diamond-mining industry and therefore the most heavily policed piece of desert in the world.

Carefully he and Harvey brought the *Mercury* seaplane in to land on the water, only to ground it on one of the many hidden sandbanks. They had covered more than 6,000 miles non-stop in just over forty-two hours. By failing to make it to Cape Town they had not broken the overall distance record but they had set the seaplane distance record. It stands to this day.

Luckily the *Mercury* was undamaged. Luckier still, the security guards at the outpost had been following reports of the record attempt on their radios and, rather than arrest them, were more than willing to help refloat them, refuel them and send them on their way to Cape Town. Imperial Airways never officially acknowledged their achievement and nor did the British government. The snub infuriated Bennett, but his reputation as an aviator had been secured. In time it would win him a vital role in the coming war, stewardship of Britain's most curious post-war airline and, in turn, command of a fleet of mighty airliners.

One of them would be called *Star Dust*.

CHAPTER THREE

WHEN HE WAS A CHILD GROWING UP IN THE 1940S, JOSÉ MOISO and his family lived close to an airbase on the outskirts of the city of Morón, an industrial suburb of Buenos Aires. Often he would stand with his father in their back garden and watch the roaring Douglas DC3s take off and land, and feel the noise of the propellers vibrating in his chest. Sometimes aluminium aircraft passed over, shining and scattering the sunlight, and he would stare upwards as if looking for his own reflection in the burnished metal. To the young José these aircraft were beautiful, thrilling even. It was only later, when his interest in aviation had shifted from childhood wonder to adult obsession, that he would identify them as having been Lancastrians. For now they were just a small boy's object of desire.

To José's parents the aircraft that rattled the pictures on their walls and so held their son's attention were only trouble. They talked of the crashes that seemed to happen so often in Argentina during the years immediately after the war, and the people killed, especially in the mountains far to the west. That would be a terrible place to crash, up there in the mountains. Surely no one could survive? They talked of one mountain crash in particular. José listened to the story over and over until it became as familiar as the nursery rhymes his parents sang to him before bed. It was the story of the golden plane, a British aircraft that crashed in the Andes loaded down with gold; gold which, if found, promised a life of blissful wealth. But it would never be found, they said, because it had also been carrying German spies from Europe to Argentina. When it crashed its mere existence had been covered up so that no one could ever find out about the Nazis on board. As to the gold, well, who knew where that was? José, the little boy from Morón, never forgot the story of the golden plane. It would drive his sense of adventure for the rest of his life.

He did eventually become a pilot, though only of private planes. His greater ambition became climbing the mountains that his parents had talked about so ominously. In his twenties he moved to the city of Mendoza, which sits in wine country on the western edge of the dusty Argentinian plain, tucked in against the foothills of the Andes. There he became a salesman, trading in electrical equipment, but wherever he was in the city he needed only to look up and he could see the mountains, by turns black, blue or grey against the clear sky. He could dream of being up there away from the bash and clatter of urban life, playing the die-hard *andinista* he was swiftly becoming. He married and started a family, upon whom he doted, but a part of him would always be elsewhere. He needed, just as the young Don Bennett had needed, an opportunity for heroism. Not to be constantly the hero; a life led like that is likely to be a short one and José was not interested in foolhardy sacrifice. But he wanted there to be, in a part of his life, the potential for admirable acts. An electrical salesman, like an Australian outback rancher, was never likely, in the pursuit of his daily duties, to receive the applause of an admiring crowd, but the great mountaineer or the great aviator always has about him the promise of the remarkable. José wanted to be remarkable.

In 1974 José Moiso finally combined his two great loves when he flew through the Andes for the first time in a glider, the idiotically light aircraft twisting and turning like a feather caught in a breeze whenever it encountered the sharp updraughts and currents that pressed their way through the stone gullies. 'Why did I do it?' he would respond to questions, his shoulders fixed in a shrug that beat off any rebuke. 'Because I was a fool. Because I wanted to have that experience. Because I wanted to fly high using the wind currents that come off the Pacific.' A year later he flew across the peaks again, this time in a pitifully under-powered light aircraft. 'And what did I discover that time?' José would ask. 'I discovered that it's very dangerous to fly over the mountains in a small machine.' It left him in no doubt. It took balls to fly in the Andes.

That same year, 1975, he climbed to his first wreck: a Douglas DC4, which had crashed 25 kilometres from Mendoza on the Cerro Pelado and which had previously been mapped. He came across the fragments of the aircraft, twisted pieces of metal, scattered across the mountainside at 15,000 feet. He found himself engrossed by the fragile relationship that exists in this part of the world between pilots and the jagged earth that lies a worryingly short distance beneath them. He decided to make it his business to search for the wrecks of aircraft lost in the Andes. He believed himself to be the perfect man for the job. People who fly over the mountains never walk in them, he announced, and people who walk in them never fly over them. José understood exactly what it took to do both. A true hero needs a niche to occupy and he had found one.

Soon his obsession became a family affair. His son Alejo climbed with him first when he was just seven years old, scaling the Arco, a 'small' hill not far from Mendoza where the young *andinistas* start out, learning how to fit their soft hands into the narrowest of cracks, and how to trick gravity into allowing them ever upwards. Alejo progressed quickly. When he was twelve he joined his father on a six-day expedition up the Cerro Plato, an impressive mountain standing over 6,000 metres high. They made the summit easily. José watched his son sucking down the thin air and relishing the pleasure of achievement, and he reached a conclusion: that moment, he would say to friends, was when he officially started getting old. He was in his mid-forties. Together Alejo and José would take on ever more complex mountains but time and again the father would find himself standing at the bottom of the rock face staring upwards as the son disappeared over the top, performing feats of mountaineering of which he himself was now incapable. He feared for his son. How could any father not? But, equally, how could he tell him to stop when it was exactly what he himself lived for? The boy was a born climber and José had no one to blame for that but himself. In 1989, aged just fifteen, Alejo became the youngest person to climb Aconcagua, the highest of the high Andes. In *andinista* circles the name Moiso had become something to reckon with.

The two of them would train all winter for the climbing they would do in the summer, until improvements in equipment meant they could climb in winter too, when there was less chance of avalanches (though the great Tupungato would always remain closed to them until the very height of summer). One year they went to the El Planchón region of the Andes in the south of Mendoza province where they were sure they would find lost wrecks. It was a place climbers rarely visited and José was certain that was the only reason nothing had ever been retrieved from there. Despite the weeks they spent searching they found nothing. They heard stories, of course, wherever they went, from the people who lived in the mountains. Some had a familiar ring to them: a plane had been found a long way up there, they said, and robbed of all that it held by local peasants who now papered the walls of their shacks with banknotes and ate off plates of gold. They said it had been lost to the thick snows which can blanket the area, or that it had become buried beneath the glacier, the bodies of the passengers and crew still intact and visible through the ice. José listened carefully to these stories, sure that one of them would provide him with the clue that would lead him to the one plane he was still desperate to find. But the stories were becoming fewer and fewer. It was only the old people in the mountains who knew them and, as time passed, they were dying. The dwindling number of young people who still lived up here so far from the life of the city weren't interested in fanciful stories about aircraft wrecks laden with riches.

To those who asked he would always say that he wanted to find the wrecks so that by mapping them he could pay tribute to the heroism of the pilots. He knew what it took to fly up there. He knew about the split-second decisions that had to be taken and the way the weather could make a fool of even the very best pilots. And it was true. He really was interested in the people who had flown in the mountains and died there. But, for all that, he could not get his parents' stories about the British plane laden with gold out of his head. Like the metal itself the tale had a gorgeous allure and it remained with him wherever he was, a motivating force that kept pushing him onward towards each new summit. As the years passed it began to seem as though that was all it would ever be: the unobtainable goal that kept José Moiso in the mountains.

And then, in October 1998, he began to hear a new set of stories: about two young climbers from Tandil who had made a curious find, high up on the slopes of Tupungato.

CHAPTER FOUR

SOME PEOPLE ARE SUITED TO WAR. THEY FUNCTION BETTER IN a world bound by orders and commands. Don Bennett was one of them. Here, in this pared-down society, his lack of social skills became a strength. He could command men with authority because he never seemed to notice what the hell they thought of him. And, of course, he had the talents that war demands. He was a master airman.

Shortly after he became prime minister, Winston Churchill appointed the great newspaper magnate Lord Beaverbrook to oversee the production of aircraft. Looking for ways to get hold of new planes quickly, Beaverbrook approved the purchase of fifty whale-bellied Hudson bombers made by the US company Lockheed. Now they had somehow to be brought across the seas from Canada. Most government officials believed the planes would have to be brought over by boat, which would take weeks, even presuming they did not fall foul of the German U-boats that now patrolled the Atlantic depths. Beaverbrook had other ideas: he believed the Hudsons should be flown across. His civil servants argued with him. Nobody had flown across the Atlantic in the winter. It simply couldn't be done. There are the unpredictable storms, the winds and the crusting wing ice. Beaverbrook overruled them. He would get young Don Bennett to do the job. He had already proven it was possible to carry freight across the north Atlantic; now he could take on a new challenge. In 1940, still just thirty years old, Bennett was appointed flying superintendent of the Atlantic Ferry Organisation flying out of Gander in Newfoundland, then a British colony.

Bennett was delighted to have been given a job suited to his talents. With his wife and their two young children he set up temporary home in Canada. He was less than impressed, however, by his bosses out in Gander. He was always less than impressed by his superiors. He simply believed he could be doing the job better than they were. Beaverbrook's man in Canada, Morris Wilson, was, Bennett announced sharply, 'devoid of qualities either good or bad'. As to many of the pilots – crop-sprayers and barnstormers, sky-writers or just plain amateurs lured in by the promise of a thousand bucks a month – they were the victims of a 'pathetic piece of bribery'. Surely, he said, better pilots could be found elsewhere? They couldn't. The RAF had none to spare and even the British Overseas Airways Corporation could supply only a dozen. This rag-tag troupe was what he had to work with. Radio operators were thin on the ground and as to navigators, well, none in this group deserved the name.

The pilots were put up in rattling old railway carriages parked in a siding, the only accommodation available at the fledgling airfield, and tested repeatedly on their flying ability and their knowledge of Morse code until Bennett was satisfied he had enough men he could trust to make the first journey. At 22.33 on 10 November 1940 the first rumbling convoy of Hudsons, seven strong in all, took off to the sound of a brass band playing 'There'll always be an England', which echoed across the denuded Newfoundland snowfields. They flew off in formation to make the night crossing of the Atlantic together, with Bennett leading. He believed himself to be the only navigator capable of keeping them on the correct heading using the few tools then available: the sextant, the moon and the stars, a worthless weather forecast and a compass; there were no radio beacons at all on this route. The convoy was instructed to follow his lead by the lights fixed at each other's tail. It was a fine plan. It might even have worked had it not been for the filthy weather they hit a few hours out. Bennett first tried to climb above it but the cloud levels were too high for there to be any hope of finding the safety of clear night sky. Reluctantly he signalled the rest of the Hudsons to break formation and attempt to keep on the track he had set them as best they could. It was not easy flying. Up there in the low oxygen atmosphere at 16,000 feet many of the pilots began to black out as the new aircraft jolted and bucked in the storm winds, only to be brought back to consciousness by the same terrible motion of the plane.

Bennett made it to Aldergrove in Ireland by 09.45 the

next morning, along with four of the formation. But four was not six and he found himself, as he would so often in the future, staring into the winter skies willing down the last aircraft in his party. He might not have held all these pilots in the very highest regard, they might not have been the men he would have chosen, but they were his pilots. He had trained them. He had sent them up there and he would wait for them to come down again – as, eventually, they did. Bennett had proven that it was possible to fly the north Atlantic in the depths of winter. In the weeks and months that followed, convoy after convoy set out from Gander to bring to Britain the aircraft it needed.

On a trip to London early in 1941, the Atlantic Ferry Organisation now fully established, he was asked to visit the directorate of bomber operations. The bombing campaign across northern Europe was progressing satisfactorily, he was told, save in one regard: the bombs that were dropped were missing their targets. Aerial photography showed harbours undamaged, factories untouched, airfields unblemished. The solution, Bennett said eventually, was a new force made up of experienced navigators. They would be the elite of the elite who would lead the bombers into the targets by marking them with flares and fireworks, something bright to light up the night sky from below. Bomber Command listened carefully to his ideas. They discussed them and then, once he had left, rejected them. The time was not yet right for valuable bombers to start dropping fireworks instead of bombs. What's more, the upper echelons of Bomber Command were certain their senior officers would not wear the idea of their best crews being creamed off to form an organization whose very existence would stand as a reproach to their dismal targeting skills.

When Bennett was eventually removed from the Atlantic Ferry Organisation – because of an increasingly familiar failure to work alongside his superiors – he did return to operational service in the RAF, though not in the new force he had proposed. For a while he kicked his heels at a training unit before being appointed wing commander to lead the bombing missions that he knew to be desperately sodden with risk.

So it proved. One night in early 1942, Ten Squadron, which he was then commanding, was dispatched to bomb the great German warship the *Tirpitz*, which was moored in a Norwegian fjord. Bennett's Halifax bomber, loaded with five 1,000-pound mines, was shot down in a barrage of anti-aircraft fire as he crossed the coast in darkness and he was forced to jump from the burning wreck as it plummeted earthwards. His parachute opened only seconds before he hit the soft, virgin snow and somehow he emerged uninjured. There was little time to wallow in the pleasure of escape. Soldiers and policemen were after him, or soon would be. It was time to make for cover. In the night shadows of a wooded stream he came across a figure hiding in the undergrowth and he pulled his gun. In his enthusiasm Bennett had almost shot his own wireless operator, who was also sheltering there. Together they made their way along railway lines to a farmhouse where they were taken in by supporters of the Norwegian Resistance. Over the next few days they were helped to escape over the mountains into neutral Sweden where Bennett was interned for a month. He was finally returned by air to the airfield at Leuchars, from where he had set off in the *Mercury* to set the seaplane record four years before. For his troubles in the snows of Scandinavia, Bennett was awarded the Distinguished Service Order. He was a bona fide war hero and he had a badge to prove it.

In the spring of 1942 Bennett was summoned to see Bert 'Bomber' Harris, who had not long taken over as head of Bomber Command. The Air Ministry had decided to adopt his targeting ideas, Harris said. An elite Pathfinder Force, under Bennett's command, was to be established. Harris wasn't at all in favour of the plan, and he told Bennett so. He knew his officers would hate the whole thing. But an order was an order and Bennett had better get on with the job. Later many would ascribe the effectiveness of Britain's bombing campaign to the revolutionary navigation and marking techniques pioneered by the Pathfinders, not least Bennett himself. His Pathfinders, he would say, turned Bomber Command 'from failure to success' although the definition of success is a contentious one. In the years since the war an increasing number of historians and commentators have argued that the carpet-bombing of German cities like Dresden and Hamburg, their terrible efficiency aided by the Pathfinders, amounted to little more than a war crime; the killing of civilians in their tens of thousands a dark and grievous stain upon the Allies' otherwise moral cause. Bennett did not see it that way. Like most of his comrades in the upper reaches of Bomber Command he believed firmly in the value and moral rightness of bombing civilian targets.

For Bennett the job brought serious perks. He was promoted from a mere wing commander to head up the Pathfinder Force, with its dozen squadrons of Lancasters, Halifaxes and Mosquitoes. (Eventually it was named Eight Group, although Bennett hated the title because he did not think it distinctive enough. They were the Pathfinder Force, he would say, or even just the PFF. Nothing else and certainly not something as banal as Eight Group.) He ended the war with the rank of air vice-marshal. For the men who volunteered, the rewards were less certain. If chosen by Bennett, and many were not, they were guaranteed a step up in rank and a pay rise, plus the right to wear the RAF eagle badge beneath their ribbons. There were to be no stars in this outfit, Bennett would say, but the message was clear: as far as the boss was concerned they were all stars, and that was why they were there. Frequently they would find themselves the victim of their bullish commander's failure to recognize that not everybody was as skilled an airman as he was. Frequently they would suffer his frustration and short temper when his grand plans foundered because they made impractical demands upon his men. But, they all agreed, he could be relied upon to defend them against critics from outside the Pathfinder Force, critics whom Bennett would swiftly dismiss as petty bureaucrats.

There was one administrator nobody could ignore, however: Bomber Harris. As these pilots were the elite, he told Bennett, they should be expected to do more than the ordinary chaps who merely carried out the bombings to the Pathfinder's targets. For Bennett's men a tour of duty would be extended from the standard thirty sorties to fifty. Bennett had long been of the opinion that bomber pilots saw more military action than any of the other services, that while a sailor at sea might engage the enemy only once or twice his men did so every time they clambered aboard their aircraft. They were, he said time and again, the very bravest of the brave. It was the kind of strident opinion that made the men under his command admire him, even if they rarely liked him. There was also a lot of truth in it. Bomber Command's losses were around 5 per cent of the aircraft dispatched on each raid, which gave the crews a one-in-twenty chance of not coming back each night. As they were originally required to fly thirty sorties, they had to buck the odds simply to survive to the end.

The fifty sorties now required of the Pathfinders clearly reduced the odds even further. After all they were the ones out in front, the very first aircraft that the German air defences would turn their guns upon. As the efficiency of the Pathfinders increased, so the Luftwaffe increased its own night-time firepower, from a few hundred fighter planes to nearly fifteen hundred, all being thrown into the air to stop Bennett's men from dropping their multi-coloured flares. The statistics bore out the risk. In August 1942, the first month of Pathfinder operations, the losses were almost 10 per cent. At Bomber Command they despaired of the Australian maverick who seemed to be losing their aircraft and killing their men. The numbers did improve, returning to the general Bomber Command average of 5 per cent, though there were some terrible nights all the same: on 1 January 1944 Bennett lost 13 per cent of his aircraft. In hard numbers those losses were vicious. Up to 600 aircraft would go out each night, many carrying half a dozen men. Of those, 50 or 60 aircraft might not return and with them would go the lives of over 300 aircrew – all in just one night.

Even Bennett, dust dry, short on jokes, long on pious demands, could not fail to be moved. At night, driving away from his headquarters at Wyton in Cambridgeshire, he sometimes pulled over to the side of the road and there in the darkness wept for the friends he had lost, invariably while following direct orders he himself had placed them under.

Since early 1942 an order had been in place barring many senior officers from taking part in active missions, in case they were shot down, taking vital operational knowledge with them. Bennett, ever suspicious of his bosses, disobeyed the order and occasionally joined a bomber crew over Germany to see for himself how successfully targets were being marked. He also insisted that his immediate subordinates went on missions from time to time. The result was inevitable: on a number of occasions the most senior officers of the Pathfinders were killed. Apart from the simple distress that these deaths caused him they also brought to the fore one particularly bizarre element of his character: a belief in the supernatural. In Gander, when aircraft of the Atlantic Ferry Organisation disappeared during the transatlantic crossings, he would regularly call the wives of the lost pilots to find out if they had any sense of whether their husbands were alive. Likewise, on one night when a senior navigation officer in the Pathfinders was lost he was delighted when the officer's identical twin brother turned up announcing that he had received a telepathic message telling him the navigator was alive and well. 'This,' Bennett reported later, 'was a truly wonderful example of the powers of telepathy at a time of great human stress.'

By the end of the war 3,618 of Bennett's Pathfinders had lost their lives during 50,490 bombing sorties. As to the men who came through, it would have been understandable if they considered themselves not merely lucky but charmed. That many of them would also ascribe an element of their survival to the great man who had commanded them through those nights of flak and bullet and air attack is also unsurprising. Despite the losses – perhaps even because of them – Bennett finished the war with a complete conviction that he understood better than anybody else the risks inherent in running a complex flying operation. Further, because of his iron confidence in his own decision-making, he believed that anybody he employed was beyond reproach. In times of war such tense emotional bonds are vital. In peacetime, however, they can be less useful. So it would prove for far too many passengers of a new airline called British South American Airways, which was to be Bennett's peacetime reward.

CHAPTER FIVE

Mendoza, Argentina

SEÑOR ATILIO BALDINI WAS A FAMILIAR SIGHT AT THE SAN
Martín library in the centre of Mendoza, where he would
go two mornings a week to riffle through aged newspaper
cuttings, yellowed with time and crumbling at their edges.
To the librarians of the San Martín there was nothing
mysterious about this small wiry man with his notebooks
and his tatty supermarket carrier-bags stuffed full of documents. Baldini was simply the plane-crash man. That was
all he ever wanted to look at: stories about plane crashes,
the ones in the mountains whose silhouette could be seen
from the street outside. If you asked him what he was doing
he would quickly tell you. Sometimes, they said, he
wouldn't stop telling you. He said that the chronicling of
plane crashes in the Andes was his life's work and there was
no reason to doubt him. By trade he was a winemaker in
one of the furrowed vineyards that ring the city and keep

the country in cheap red wine made from the malbec grape. By obsession he was an aviation historian and a self-trained one at that. 'I do not have a cell phone or a computer,' he declared with undisguised pride when asked about his methods, his face breaking into a wide grin. 'It is just me with my notebooks.'

He might have liked the life of a pilot but he could only swim so hard against the current of his family's history. In 1937 his mother's brother, Guillermo, was killed in a military plane crash. Guillermo's parents had warned him against going into the air force: 'You'll end up dead,' they said. In the Baldini family it is said that Guillermo's father – Atilio's grandfather – died of a broken heart. A life in flying was never going to be open to Atilio, however much he might have wished it.

'When you are forbidden to go into something you become more curious,' he says. Living in the shadow of the mountains and with the memory of his uncle's death etched upon his mind, he became intrigued by the stories that lay up there. He decided he would record them. By the mid-1980s he had his first chronicle. It listed just a couple of dozen lost aircraft, starting in 1919 with that delicate Newport of Benjamin Matienzo and working forward to the present day. It was, he says now, only a work in progress. In time it came to list sixty-six wrecks on the Argentinian side of the Andes. In 1985, shortly after the first draft was completed, Atilio showed it to his friend, Gustavo Marón, then just a college student in Mendoza but also someone who shared his passion. Marón had already edited magazines about air crashes and aviation around Mendoza and, although he would go on to study and practise law, his fascination would remain with him. They made an odd couple, these two: Baldini, the shambling winemaker with his pockets full of documents; Marón, the careful and cautious small-town lawyer almost half Baldini's age, his shoes polished to a shine, his hair combed just so. Something about the partnership worked.

'I became an investigator because of Atilio,' Marón says today. 'He is my mentor and I am his student.' Later, when questions were raised over who had found what and when on Tupungato, the air-crash investigators of the Argentinian air force heaped praise on the research work of Marón and Baldini. Without them – without Baldini's endless hours in the San Martín library and Marón's obsessive attention to detail – the wreckage may never have been identified. No one else had kept such complete records of the aircraft that had crashed in the Andes.

In 1985 that first version of Baldini's chronicle made an impression on Marón. At number four or five on the list was exactly the kind of mystery he adored: an aircraft crewed by former members of the British Royal Air Force which had disappeared over the Andes on 2 August 1947. Baldini had only two other pieces of information. On board was a British diplomat, he reported, and the plane had gone missing somewhere to the north of Mendoza. The entry also made mention of press reports speculating that the plane had gone right over the top of the mountains and crashed into the Pacific. In the years that followed Marón would be able to find out only a little more: that the aircraft was a Lancastrian – a civilian conversion of the legendary

Lancaster bomber; that it had been operated by an airline called British South American Airways, and that it was called *Star Dust*. None of this, useful as it was, provided any clues as to where the wreckage could be. And so it would remain until a November day in 1998 when Marón received a telephone call at his law offices on avenida 25 de Mayo, not too far from the central court building in Mendoza.

The call was from José Moiso. They had been introduced only a few months before, by a mutual friend. In a town as relatively small and tight-knit as Mendoza it was always likely that a man who searched for aircraft wrecks on the mountainsides and a man who searched for them on paper would eventually meet. Now José wanted some help: he had been told about a new crash site in the Andes and he was wondering whether Marón might be able to identify the aircraft from the sketchy details in his possession.

José was lucky to have heard about the find at all. Pablo Reguera and Fernando Garmendia came down off Tupungato in early February 1998, flushed with success at having finally completed the climb and deposited their plaque in memory of Vierio and Rabal. The first person they saw was the soldier in charge of the mules they had hired from the army mountain station. He all but laughed when they told him about the fragments of aircraft they had found: the engine and those strips of pinstripe. Lots of people went up Tupungato each year, the soldier said. Why should they suddenly find a wreck if it had been lying there for years? They must have been mistaken.

They were more fortunate with Sergeant Armando

Cardozo, who was also up at the station that day. Though the man himself would have denied it – certainly to his commanding officers – climbers who knew him saw Sergeant Cardozo as an *andinista* first and a soldier second. He had lived in these mountains all his life and he knew them better than almost anybody else. Where most experienced climbers might reach the summit of Tupungato once in their lives Sergeant Cardozo had already done it three times. He was tall and dark, solidly built and not given easily to idle talk. It suited him, this life with the Eleventh Mountain Regiment of the army's Eighth Mountain Brigade, where he could spend as much time as possible out on the silent peaks listening to the wind. He certainly did not dismiss Reguera and Garmendia's story. He had been around the mountains long enough to know that they could easily turn up the unexpected and unfound. Still, there was not much he could do with the information apart from ask other climbers, as they passed through, whether they had seen anything. It did not help that the climbers from Tandil had failed to record the location; Tupungato was a big mountain.

It was many months later, when the Argentinian summer had given way to winter and winter had in turn become spring, that Sergeant Cardozo sat down for lunch with José Moiso at the army barracks near the town of Tupungato, a few miles away from the mountain station. The barracks, which also takes its name from the mountain that overshadows it, was not the most comfortable of places for José to break bread. Few Argentinians can forget that the military was responsible for governing the country during the far-right rule of the generals in Argentina between 1976 and 1983. Over 30,000 people 'disappeared' at the hands of the junta during those years, apparently because of leftist sympathies. But this was a different age, and anyway José and the officers around him had something in common: a shared love of the mountains at their door. He avoided politics, as Argentinians so often do, and instead talked about the wrecks he had been looking for and the wrecks he had found. Sergeant Cardozo listened closely. He told José about the find that had been reported to him almost nine months before. José was intrigued, particularly by the words etched on to the engine the two climbers had come across: Rolls-Royce was still one of the most famous names in aviation engines.

Gustavo Marón was intrigued too because to his certain knowledge only three aircraft lost in the Andes had been powered by engines made by Rolls-Royce. One of those was the most famous Andean plane crash of them all; more famous, even, than the golden plane. On 12 October 1972 a Fairchild FH–227 left Montevideo, the capital of Uruguay, carrying fifteen members of the Old Christians' Club, an amateur rugby team made up of former pupils from one of the country's most prestigious private boys' Catholic schools. To bring down the cost to each team member of chartering the aircraft, they were accompanied by twenty-five of their friends and family, who paid their way. Together they were bound for a match in Santiago, Chile, a flight of some 900 miles that would take them out over the Andes. A little way into the journey the pilots, both members of the Uruguayan air force, received word that Pacific winds were clashing with waves of air flooding in from the Argentinian plain, causing extreme turbulence over the mountains. They were not at all convinced that the relatively light propeller-driven Fairchild would be a match for the buffeting and blows they would receive up there. They put down in Mendoza for the night, where the passengers stocked up on cigarettes and alcohol and a little chocolate. The next day, a Friday the thirteenth, they were told on their radios by a pilot who had just flown over the peaks that the Fairchild would have little trouble. Despite their misgivings, and with much urging and taunting from their passengers, the air force officers agreed to make the trip.

It was the wrong decision. Soon smothered by cloud and flying on instruments, the aircraft hit turbulence that thumped them down 3,000 feet in a matter of seconds. The passengers had a moment to study the awesome sight of the mountainside only a few feet beyond their window before it ripped off the wing, which in turn ripped off the tail, leaving a gaping hole. Three of the rugby players and two of the crew were dragged out into the mountain air still strapped into their seats and then what was left of the air-craft hit the snow slopes, skidding downwards at 200 miles per hour. The shattered remains came to rest on a snowfield at 12,000 feet. There were, initially, thirty-two survivors from the original forty-five on board.

If they had hoped for, or expected, rescue they were to be disappointed. They were miles off course and the white-painted plane made an impossible target to find amid the glistening snow. Hours turned into days and days turned into weeks and, as cold and hunger bit deep, more and more of their number succumbed, their bodies lying frozen and preserved in the snow and ice around them. A little chocolate bought in the boutiques of Mendoza could not sustain them here against the elements. Eventually, sheltering in the fragile safety of the wrecked fuselage, the survivors realized that some of them would have to go and find help but that, to do so, they would first have to eat. They also realized that the only source of food was the bodies of their friends and family lying all about them. Many of the survivors were staunchly Catholic; they debated furiously the morality of resorting to cannibalism in order to survive. A number argued that it would be a sin in God's eyes simply to fade away when here provided was a route to salvation, and in any case the souls had long departed these corpses. Finally reconciled, they took to eating the bodies, tentatively at first, but with more vigour as time went by. Pieces would be cut from the frozen cadavers where they lay in the snow and then thawed out in the sun before either being cooked or eaten raw. Most of those who did eat survived. There is no doubt that it provided the final means of escape: the human flesh was a vital source of energy for three of the men who, ten weeks after the crash, stumbled down the mountain and found rescue for them all. There were sixteen survivors.

The story of the Uruguayan rugby team, which became a bestselling book and later a less impressive film, both called *Alive!*, also became a modern legend in and around the Andes and no more so than in the town of Mendoza where the plane stopped over for its last night. It was proof of what a bitter foe the Andes could be, both for the aircraft above them and for the people on the ground.

Marón thought immediately of this plane. The Fairchild FH–227 had been fitted with two Rolls-Royce engines. But he also knew that whatever engine Reguera and Garmendia had found, and wherever they had found it, it could not belong to the rugby club's plane. Twenty-six years on, everybody knew where that wreck was. It was part of mountain folklore.

That left two aircraft. One of those was a Canadair CL–44, which also disappeared in 1972 and which had been fitted with four Rolls-Royce Tyne motors. Officially it was never found but in 1982 two Spanish climbers came across a wheel, two lifejackets and part of a fuselage on the south face of Aconcagua. It was now generally accepted that those pieces of wreckage belonged to the Canadair.

That left just the one aircraft: a Lancastrian, fitted with four Rolls-Royce Merlins, which disappeared on 2 August 1947. If there really was a Rolls-Royce aircraft engine lying somewhere in the mountains close to Mendoza it had to belong to the Lancastrian, Marón said. José was overjoyed because he was in no doubt. The Lancastrian was the golden plane that his parents had talked of so often when he was a child. Curiously, however hard Marón tried, however hard he asked, José was unwilling to tell him where exactly this piece of wreckage was. He would not name the mountain. He would not even give the rough location. He would only say that it was up there. Waiting.

CHAPTER SIX

THE EUROPEAN WAR WAS COMING TO AN END, GERMANY WAS being defeated, and Don Bennett needed a new job. Something big. Something a man in a hurry could get his teeth into. At the invitation of the Liberal Party, who fancied having a war hero on their side, he tried his hand at politics and was elected Liberal member of Parliament for Middlesbrough in the north-east. It wasn't as great a personal triumph as it sounds. By convention the political parties did not stand against each other at by-elections during the war and Bennett was elected unopposed. He was swiftly turfed out in the post-war Labour landslide of July 1945.

So not politics then. And not the military: he was done with that. No, it would have to be civilian aviation, just as it had been before the war when he pioneered the freight route across the north Atlantic. Only this time the challenge would come from the south Atlantic. While long-haul services to South Africa and Australia were operating before the Second World War, the routes to South America had remained relatively untouched by the dynamic hand of commerce. That was hardly surprising: as far as the great aviation pioneers were concerned the north Atlantic, with its bustling cosmopolitan cities on either shore, was the more dashing and glamorous proposition. It was not until 1927, a full eight years after Alcock and Brown made their non-stop crossing of the north, that a French crew bothered to complete an east–west crossing on the southern path, from St Louis in Senegal to Natal in Brazil. It was the logical route: both towns were perched on the humps of each continent as if they were reaching out to each other. The distance was just 1,890 miles, a hundred miles less than the distance across the north Atlantic.

The commercial aviation that did exist in the 1930s was restricted mostly to postal services operated by fledgling European carriers such as Air France and Deutsche Lufthansa, which still had to rely on ships to carry the cargo for the Atlantic stretch of the journey to South America. The one passenger service by aircraft was operated haltingly from 1939 by an Italian carrier owned by Mussolini's family but that, like everything else, came to an end in 1941 for the duration of the war. As early as March 1938, however, the British government's Cadman Committee on Aviation argued that Britain should set up a service to South America given the long-established cultural ties with the region, in particular with Argentina. Early in 1945, with the war edging towards a conclusion, five

British shipping lines – the Booth Steamship Company, the Vestey Steamship Company, the Royal Mail Shipping Company, the Pacific Steam Navigation Company and the Blue Star Line – came together to form British Latin American Air Lines Limited. John Booth of the Booth Steamship Company was appointed chairman. The shipping firms could see the way the wind was blowing. The increasing use of air power in the war had convinced them that aviation was the coming thing. If they didn't embrace it now, in peacetime it would surely kill them off as swiftly as a 1,000-pound mine from the belly of a Lancaster. They had the managers and the ticketing infrastructure in place at the relevant ports. What's more they understood the business. So what if it was by air rather than sea? It all amounted to the same thing.

They did not get the chance to prove it. In March 1945 the British government announced that post-war civil aviation would be taken into public ownership. There would be three corporations. British European Airways (BEA) would run domestic and European services. The pre-existing British Overseas Airways Corporation (BOAC) would handle routes to the Commonwealth, USA, China and the Far East. Finally, the new British Latin American Air Lines would be renamed British South American Airways (BSAA) and given control of all the routes across the south Atlantic. For the old hands in BOAC who, with some justification, considered themselves to be best equipped to run long-haul services, this was not welcome news. They wanted South America as well. But the Air Ministry stood firm. BSAA would be a separate company and its head of operations would be Don Bennett, who had served them all so well during his command of the Pathfinders. Bennett was not at all surprised by the intervention of BOAC, which he already distrusted. They represented everything that was wrong with British corporatism: slow and flabby, he would say, they operated at a loss and functioned under the dead hand of bureaucracy. It infuriated him that the first test flight to South America to check the viability of the proposed route was undertaken in October 1945 by a BOAC pilot and aircraft because BSAA was not ready to do it themselves.

For a man who had never before run an airline, indeed had never even been in a management position with an airline, there were a lot of choices to be made, not least among them which aircraft to operate. For Bennett that was not difficult. In 1943 the Canadian air force made a few adjustments to a number of Lancaster bombers so they could carry post, freight and eventually passengers across the north Atlantic. Two years later A.V. Roe Ltd, British manufacturer of the great bomber, was making the adjustments itself and marketing it as the Avro 691 Lancastrian. Off came the wart-like gun turret on its spine. The gun positions on the nose and tail were also removed and the nose lengthened to make extra space for carrying cargo. The grey-green camouflage colours of wartime were replaced with a shiny metallic skin and, inside, space was made for thirteen passengers, six on one side and seven on the other. For A.V. Roe the venture made commercial sense. At the end of the war it was impossible simply to halt military production. Lancaster bombers kept rolling off the production line long after they were needed. Many would be completed then moved to another workshop where the recently installed engines would be sawn off and the rest of the brand new, unflown aircraft sent for shimmering scrap. The Lancastrian presented a solution, though it, too, swiftly reached obsolescence. While nearly 7,400 Lancaster bombers were built during the war only eighty-two Lancastrians – a small number by the standards of commercial aircraft manufacture – ever emerged from the workshops of A.V. Roe.

For Bennett the appeal of the Lancastrian was more emotional than practical. The Lancaster bomber had carried so many of his boys safely. It was the warhorse upon which so much had depended. He was certain he could depend on it again now. Most importantly, it was British. Australian he might have been, but Bennett was nevertheless a zealous British patriot to the very pit of his RAF-flat stomach. He sneered at the lousy management of BOAC who had opted for 'foreign rubbish' like the American Douglas Skymasters. That was an act of gross betrayal. It mattered not at all that the Lancastrian was a noisy and, in many ways, uneconomical aircraft. It was irrelevant that the Skymasters would be better suited to long-haul flying, or that they looked like civilian airliners, whereas the Lancastrians just looked like a shiny version of the box-like crate that had bombed the hell out of the enemy for the last few years. The Lancastrian was British, and the government was encouraging consumers to buy British now that the war was over and the economy was struggling to get back on its feet. Bennett believed in leading from the front. He had always done so and he would do so now. He swiftly – and proudly – accepted the order for six of the Mark 3s which the Air Ministry, in charge of procurement for the airlines, had made on their behalf. (Later BSAA would add a dozen Avro Yorks to their fleet, a plane which was also a development of the original Lancaster bomber. It had a new fuselage which could seat twenty-one passengers, though a shorter range than the Lancastrian.)

Who would fly them? An airline needed pilots with airline experience but they were few and far between, not least because BOAC had grabbed a lot of their old staff back as they came out of the RAF. Bennett was to have just two, Gordon Store and David Brice, both of whom had flown with Imperial Airways and, later, Bennett's Atlantic Ferry Organisation. They took up senior positions in the company. As to the rest, well, that wouldn't be a problem. After all, Bennett had just spent four years running a flying operation staffed by the very elite of British aviation. The only difference between what his boys had been required to do then and what they would need to do now was that they wouldn't be shot at. They wouldn't have to drop flares and markers every time they reached their destination, they'd just have to land: simple stuff for a Pathfinder. So he invited them to join him and many, looking for a berth in civil aviation, said a swift yes. There was tall, imposing Cliff Alabaster, master navigator, who'd flown around a hundred sorties during the war in various roles. There was Frank Taylor, who'd completed eighty-two. There was Reginald Cook and 'Crackers' Cracknell and, as medical adviser, 'Doc' MacGowan, who had performed the same function for Bennett in wartime. In total there were twelve captains and fifteen first officers hired to roll out the airline, and all but a couple were former Pathfinders. Eventually sixty former Pathfinders would work for BSAA. In the months immediately after the war visitors to the airline's headquarters at 19 Grafton Street in London's Mayfair – telephone number REGent 4141 – would find a civilian building with a curiously military atmosphere. Staff were referred to by their RAF ranks, not least Bennett himself who was, and would remain, AVM (air vice-marshal) throughout his stewardship. In those first few months many of the pilots, who were still serving officers merely seconded from the RAF at that point, were also to be seen striding about the corridors in military uniform. The BSAA uniforms hadn't arrived and they didn't have anything else to wear.

The military culture was not a problem as far as Bennett was concerned. BSAA was to be a very different operation from the others, he told his men, and that sort of thing set them apart. They would get the job done in their way. Over at BOAC new recruits from the RAF were being sent on courses to bring them up to the standards required by civil aviation. Bennett was invited to send his men on these courses too but he flatly refused, believing it was entirely unnecessary. The training captain at BOAC wrote and asked him to think again. 'May I entreat you not to allow the standards of qualifications for commercial civil aviation aircrew to be lowered,' he said.

Bennett replied swiftly. 'I would stress that our

requirements are higher than those of BOAC, not lower,' he wrote. 'Our crews will come direct to us and undergo a short course in this company before starting the survey flights.'

In one respect what Bennett said was true. For a pilot to be in command at BSAA he had first to hold a full navigator's licence. But this was only because, unlike BOAC, Bennett didn't want to employ extra navigators as part of the crew. He wanted the pilots to do the job. It would save money, and he was determined that his airline would operate at a profit. Further, because of how little time there was before they had to start services, some of the second officers he hired had none of the basic navigation qualifications for civil aviation, nor did they have licences to fly Lancastrians. Bennett told them they would have to pass their exams in their own time and within six months. As to gaining licences on the aircraft they would be flying, they were told they would have to perform six landings. The problem was there weren't enough planes or enough routes being flown to give these lesser recruits the opportunity. Often the requirement simply went by the board during that first year.

Back at BOAC a training officer was surveying his latest bunch of ex-RAF recruits. 'It is my job,' he told them, 'to turn you gallant young gentlemen into fussy old women.' Nobody was employed to do that at BSAA: it was a company of heroes.

That's how Bennett liked to operate. He trusted his men, however they came to be in his employ. In the early days of BSAA he went to Buenos Aires to start promoting his new company. Archie Jackson, a young Anglo-Chilean pilot who was then flying with the Chilean state airline Lan Chile, heard that Bennett was there, staying at the Plaza Hotel. He turned up as the boss was concluding a press conference and asked him to consider taking him on. After all, Jackson said, he was a civilian pilot, he knew the region and he spoke Spanish.

Bennett looked him up and down.

'Had any crashes?' he said.

'No, sir,' Jackson said.

Bennett nodded. Jackson would do. He served his notice with Lan Chile and joined BSAA soon after.

It had aircraft. It had pilots. All BSAA needed now was an airport from which to operate. Bennett knew exactly which one he wanted: out to the west of London was a new airfield still in the throes of development. There were no buildings to speak of or hangars for that matter but in time it would prove itself, Bennett was sure of that. The only immediate problem was the condition of the runway, which was covered with builders' materials. One morning in December 1945 he turned up to survey it. He was immediately stopped by the building foreman who wanted to know what he was doing there. Bennett asked if, in exchange for a few quid, he could get the runway cleared. The foreman agreed that it could be done. The next day Bennett flew down from the A.V. Roe factory at Waddington in the first of the Lancastrians. There was no one manning the control tower that day because the control tower had not yet been built. Bennett simply looked out of the window to find his way to the airfield. Once down he went immediately to the Air Ministry in the centre of London and baldly announced to the civil servant in charge that he was ready to start services from the new airfield. The official demurred. BSAA was listed to fly from Hurn, near Bournemouth on the south coast. And in any case the London airfield wasn't ready for aircraft. Yes it was, Bennett said. He'd just landed there. And as he'd have to take off again, the service might as well start from there.

The weary official agreed. Bennett had contrived to make BSAA the very first airline to operate out of that new London airfield which, in just a few years, would become known as Heathrow.

It had been a tough few months but, as he prepared for that first flight, Bennett could feel a certain amount of satisfaction at a job well done. What he couldn't see was where his crew of frighteningly brave ex-bomber pilots flying only British kit with their eyes set on profit would eventually lead him. He was already the first man to fly cargo across the north Atlantic. He was the holder of the seaplane distance record. He had turned Bomber Command from failure to success. Finally, he was on course for another achievement. In BSAA, his very own Bomber Command in mufti, Bennett had created what would eventually become the most dangerous airline in the western world.

CHAPTER SEVEN

ON A WINTER'S NIGHT AT THE BEGINNING OF THE TWENTY-FIRST century a Boeing 747–400 in the colours of British Airways takes off from Gatwick Airport to the south of London, bound for Buenos Aires. It is quiet here tonight. There is just one other flight departing after this, a non-stop service to Zimbabwe, but earlier in the day airliners were taking off and landing every sixty seconds. Those that arrived too early for their landing slot, or found themselves in a queue when they got here, were put into a holding pattern above southern England so that the air space bristled with thousands of tonnes of aircraft chasing each other's tails at hundreds of miles an hour. There was nothing special about today. It is always like this above Gatwick Airport at the beginning of the twenty-first century.

Now the 747 – call sign Speedbird 2267 – is cleared for take-off. It weighs 392.4 tonnes, which is 4.5 tonnes below its maximum take-off weight. Of that, 163.2 tonnes is fuel, carried in eight tanks. Three are in each wing, one is in the belly and one in the nose. The rest of the weight is the aircraft itself, the 375 passengers, the 16 cabin crew, the 4 pilots up on the flight deck and the cargo. It is 70.7 metres long and 19.3 metres high. The fuselage is 6.4 metres wide and the wingspan is 64.9 metres. Beneath those wings are four Rolls-Royce RB211–524H engines. Each is capable of producing 60,300 pounds of thrust. Each is equivalent to 120,000 horses thundering down the runway. That is what you need to accelerate 392.4 tonnes of aircraft to an average take-off speed of 207 miles per hour.

For the passengers the comfort of their flight will depend on none of this for, at the beginning of the twenty-first century, the technical sophistication of aviation is a given. It will depend instead upon whether they turned left or right as they walked on to the aircraft. Those who turned left will have been heading for club class or, better still, first class. There are just fourteen first-class passengers tonight, right up in the nose, who will be able to sleep flat in fatly upholstered seats that turn into beds. They will be offered dishes designed by one of Britain's greatest chefs – lime-marinated crab with seared prawns and mango to start, followed by cracked-pepper-crusted fillet steak. They will, if they care to, drink *grand cru* Chablis and, when they are done, they will watch their own choice of films on their own individual video player. For this they will have paid around £8,000 return. In club class the fifty-five passengers, who have paid roughly two-thirds of the first-class price, will have slightly less room and a little less flexibility on the menu but even so fillet steak and carpaccio of tuna will be theirs for the asking. The remaining 332 passengers who turned right into economy class will have paid no more than £600 and will be served lemon-glazed chicken breast for dinner. They will watch their films and try to get some sleep in their narrow seats. And all the passengers will worry, although not about machine safety. Nobody worries about mechanical failure these days, for the odds are in their favour. They will worry instead about other, newer threats. Following the events in New York of 11 September 2001, whose terrible echoes will be heard for years to come, they may wonder whether a terrorist with a death wish might be aboard their flight, even though the odds are also in their favour. Or those in cramped seating will look inwards and worry about fatal blood clots, produced by hours of constricted posture, surging upwards to plug their heart or lungs.

Up on the flight deck the two pilots working the first shift face banks of computer screens telling them exactly what the aircraft they are in charge of is doing. They have constant read-outs of the oxygen being pumped into the cabins to keep them pressurized and they know all about the hydraulics and the electrics. That is their job. They are not there to fly the plane, unless it is strictly necessary to do so. They are there to monitor the plane flying itself. There are two weather radars, which hunt the night sky for fronts, and a de-icing system which turns on automatically the moment it detects crusting on the wing. They will be in radio contact with the ground for the entirety of the flight save for forty-five minutes far off Dakar in West Africa, but even then the global positioning system will still be keeping them on track. The plane's route will be beamed back to them from a series of satellites miles above the earth and marked by a glowing red line across a dark screen. Six hours into the thirteen-hour flight the first crew will retire to the two-bedded room up behind the cockpit and get some sleep while the second crew takes over. Finally, as they come in to land at Buenos Aires, the pilots will decide to stick with the autopilot. Using a series of radio aids on the ground, pre-set programmes and a computer calibrated to the parameters of this exact aircraft, it will land the plane for them, perfectly.

There was no autopilot capable of landing the shining Lancastrian, registration G–AGWG, that stood waiting on the edge of the west London airfield on the morning of 1 January 1946. Nor were there bunks for the pilots. Don Bennett himself would be captain on this flight, the very first by BSAA, and he wasn't about to take a nap on the job, even though there would be no possibility of sleep until Rio, thirty-four hours and four flights away. The plane weighed 29.5 tonnes fully loaded, or just 7.5 per cent of that 747 over half a century later. It was 23.4 metres long and had a wingspan of 31 metres. Like those of the 747, the engines were made by Rolls-Royce, but these were 73 times less mighty: they were Merlin T24s, capable of just 1,640 horsepower each. That was all you needed to get an aircraft weighing 29.5 tonnes to its take-off speed of 150 miles per hour.

That first aircraft was called *Starlight*. All BSAA planes would be called *Star* something, either as one word or two. It was their brand. The logo was a stylized art-deco 'starman' of angles and points: arms back, chin up, hair trailing as it flew east into the wind (even though, from Britain, the aircraft themselves flew west). It was there on the notepaper and the timetables and even on the nose of each plane, on the side just forward of the cockpit. The motto was 'Fly with the stars'. Even the stewardesses were called Stargirls. On this flight it was a young woman called Mary Guthrie, for whom the job was a bit of a comedown given her expertise. During the war she had been a pilot, ferrying aircraft between workshops and airfields. Now, in peacetime, she had to take what she could get, and upper-class skivvying for BSAA at least promised travel and had a certain cinematic glamour.

It didn't promise comfort. The cabin was just 1.82 metres wide and 1.9 metres high. At the front, behind the flight deck, was a cramped galley from where the girls, sometimes in pairs, usually working alone, were to serve defrosted meals called 'Frood', which had been prepared by the Lyons Tea House company. It was, the Stargirls would all eventually agree, pretty foul stuff. Most of them would avoid eating the hideous versions of chicken à la king or veal blanquette prepared for the passengers. Instead they made do with endless cups of tea sweetened with condensed milk, or the soup and orange juice which they carried in vacuum flasks for the passengers. At first washing up the china – and it always was china – was a chore. There was just a sink with cold water and no detergent, nor anywhere to put the dishes when they were done. Only later would the company start offloading the unwashed crockery at each stopover. As to drink, there was a box bar containing spirits plus a good supply of raw Chilean red wine which, for some reason, the passengers didn't appreciate. As time passed and the flights became routine, some of the more worldly Stargirls took to finishing off the bottles in the galley during the endlessly dull stretches when there was nothing to do, filling their mouths with peppermints afterwards to hide the smell.

And then there were the opportunities for free enterprise. The Stargirls and crew were paid their expenses at the rate of 17 Argentinian pesos to the pound, but in the change shops of Buenos Aires you could get a rate of 10 pesos. Those with Spanish and initiative in equal measure would make for the change shops to cash up the moment they landed. When BSAA routes extended to the West Indies one Stargirl called Jean Fowler, an Anglo-Argentinian who had taken the job to avoid going back to teaching after years in the women's auxiliary air force, discovered there was profit to be made elsewhere. She could pick up bottles of Johnny Walker and Black Label whisky in the grocery shops of Bermuda for five shillings. She then resold them in the nightclubs of Santiago, Chile, for the equivalent of £8. She bought beautifully stitched crocodile handbags, just the one a trip, to be resold in Britain at a massive profit, and even a fur coat, which she claimed to British customs was her own. Half a century later she looks back at her life of petty crime, shifting contraband back and forth across the borders of Latin America, with curiosity. 'Frankly I don't know why every girl didn't do it,' she says. 'It was so simple. But then they didn't all have a lot of gumption.' To work as a Stargirl for BSAA you had to be unmarried and of 'a certain class'. The airline only wanted what they defined as 'nice girls' and while some like Jean had come to adulthood during the curious freedoms of the war, for many others BSAA was their first job after leaving home. They would no sooner have taken to a little bit of smuggling on the side than they would have sworn in church.

For the passengers the experience boasted fewer perks. Even though it was weeks faster than making the trip to Argentina by ship, it was a strenuous journey that lasted three days, complete with occasional night stops in bizarre French colonial outposts that still held their ground in the African bush or in tumbledown hotels on Brazil's coastal fringe. (The Stargirls were told to pack Keating's Powder to kill fleas and ticks in their rooms in West Africa. They also took toilet paper, and a torch to help them find their way to outside lavatories. Finally they packed a ball of string, to be stretched out across the room as a hanger for clothes. If their uniforms were hung in the wardrobes, cockroaches would make for the first slick of perspiration and stay there. The passengers received none of this insider advice.) As to the Lancastrians they paid to travel in, they were only nominally soundproofed so that the engines roared at them for hours on end. The only protection they were given were wads of cotton-wool to be stuffed in the ears, handed out at take-off, along with a boiled sweet (to be sucked, rather than pushed in after the cotton wool). There was no pressurization, which could lead to dizziness or head-aches at altitudes of up to 10,000 feet. Thereafter the Lancastrians were equipped with limited oxygen which the passengers took through a tube as they rose up over 20,000 feet to clear the Andes. For this the well-heeled passengers paid £352 return, equivalent to £8,000 today, almost exactly the same price as that first-class ticket on the British Airways' Boeing 747–400.

For the pilots the equipment was basic, but then they were used to that. There were only two real navigational aids: a 'twitcher', which held two needles on a dial that would cross when the Lancastrian was over a radio beacon, giving the pilots a fix on the nearby runway, and a distance-measuring device called Eureka. There were other pieces of useful kit coming on to the market, including a radio compass, but Bennett refused to use it because it was American. (When A.V. Roe delivered new aircraft with the compass pre-fitted Bennett simply ordered that it be stripped out.) Pilots were expected to use their old navigational skills instead, even if it meant dropping below cloud over the Atlantic to calculate drift caused by the wind from the way the peaks of the ocean waves were moving. For Bennett's crew these stipulations merely emphasized how much faith the boss had in them.

'As far as we were concerned Bennett was a wartime hero,' says Archie Jackson today. 'He took an awful lot of chances and they always seemed to work for him.'

Don Mackintosh, who joined BSAA from the special duties squadrons that had been responsible for the famed Dambuster operations, felt the same way. 'Bennett simply said, "You are good lads, you came through the war. You have my complete confidence." The expectation was there that you would go to the limits, that you would press on.

People found it familiar because it was the way it had worked in the war.'

For that first trip, though, Bennett himself was in command and he would be responsible for all the pressing on. He lined up with his first and second officers, Wing Commanders Cracknell and Alabaster, and the rest of the crew, for an official photograph. He listened solemnly as the aviation minister, Lord Winster, paid tribute to 'this beautiful aircraft' while some of the men gave each other long sideways looks. Buffed metal skin aside, it was still only an old Lancastrian. No matter. At 12.07 they were on their way, complete with nine non-paying passengers, most of whom were the wing commanders and squadron leaders who would be the BSAA representatives at each airfield and who needed dropping off. They made it to the Portuguese capital five and a quarter hours later and then, nine hours after that, to the Yundum airfield at Bathurst in Gambia where, when there were paying passengers on board, the crew would swap with a fresh team of pilots and radio officers. But not on this trip. Flight-time restrictions on pilots were a thing of the future. At 05.10, just an hour after arriving, they were off again for the eight-hour crossing of the Atlantic to Natal in Brazil, where they were met at the steps by stewards holding platters of fresh pineapple and jugs of freshly squeezed orange juice. For most of those on board it was a sudden and glorious culture shock. After six years of war, of food rationing and cold and gloom that turned the world a dismal monochrome, they had arrived in a South America that had known none of this. It was a place where fresh fruit was plentiful, where the skies were the deepest shade of hot blue, where palm trees rustled in the breeze.

It was a paradise that was almost lost as soon as it was gained. In Rio de Janeiro, the next stop, Bennett wanted to land at Galeão airfield, partly because it was at the back of the Rio harbour and therefore close to the centre of town, and partly because he did not think the runway was long enough at the alternative airfield, Santos Dumont, some distance away. But the Brazilians were furiously protective of their military installations and refused. It had to be Santos Dumont, where the runway ran into the sea at both ends. A furious Bennett brought the Lancastrian down, with Alabaster sitting nervously beside him as co-pilot. Cracknell, who had been navigating, was standing up between them, staring anxiously out at the runway as they now careered towards its end.

'Swing it,' he said suddenly, as they roared onwards. 'Swing it round or we'll end up in the water.'

Bennett ignored him and brought *Starlight* to a juddering halt just yards from the water's edge, without saying a word.

Immediately he went to the Brazilian air ministry and informed them that it would be impossible to get the Lancastrian off the ground at Santos Dumont if it was fully loaded. The runway wasn't long enough. They would have to unload everything, fly down to Galeão, reload and take off from there. If, that was, the Brazilian government wanted an air service from Britain. Grudgingly the Brazilians agreed. The next morning the Lancastrian's cargo was moved over to a DC3 for the short hop from

Santos Dumont and Bennett decided to go with it, while others piloted the empty Lancastrian. Shortly before the DC3 took off, Mary Guthrie went through the aircraft checking everybody was wearing their seatbelts. Bennett was not and she suggested he put his on.

'I most certainly will not,' he barked. 'Seatbelts have caused many accidents. In fact they have caused more casualties than they have prevented.' Guthrie was not about to argue. You did not argue with AVM Bennett. After all, he clearly knew what he was doing. Hadn't he just pulled off that remarkable landing?

So it seemed as BSAA chalked up an almost spotless safety record – for all of nine months.

CHAPTER EIGHT

The Passengers – Part I

FOR CASIS SAID ATALAH THE NEWS THAT ARRIVED IN SANTIAGO early in 1947 was less than welcome. It was not simply that his mother was ill. It grieved him terribly that he had not seen her since the day in 1914 when, still a teenager, he left his family's home town of Bethlehem to join his brothers in Latin America. Of course he wanted to see her before she died, as the letter from relatives in Palestine said she soon would. But life was complicated now. He had done well for himself here in Chile, as had so many other members of the family. He was the boss of a fine millinery company that imported hats from the greatest manufacturers in Italy and Switzerland and France. He sold fashion to the ladies of Santiago and they, in turn, made him wealthy. There was his wife, Lola, and his five children, Eduardo, Nazir, Issa, Mario and Maria. The eldest, Eduardo, was only 11. Maria was not yet a year old. How could he leave them behind while he disappeared off halfway around the world for months on end?

He went to see his older brother Nicolas and pleaded with him to go in his place. Yes, he was well aware that Nicolas had already been back to Palestine. But his children were grown up now. Nicolas did not have the responsibilities that weighed down upon Casis, who feared flying and the dangers it carried in those chaotic years that followed the war. But Nicolas was having none of it. He had been to Palestine once. This time it was the turn of his younger brother.

Casis accepted defeat. He would have to go. A week before he left in the spring of 1947 he arranged for a photograph to be taken of the entire family so that his mother could see her grandchildren for the first time. He appears in it at the centre, a big round-shouldered man with a solid jaw and a thinning slick of hair, wearing a suit of old pinstripe with wide lapels. In the lining of the suit he wore for the trip – perhaps the same one as he wore for the photograph; even the most accomplished of men had a limited wardrobe – was stitched a diamond, for emergencies. In his luggage he carried a large painting of the Virgin Mary, a mark of his devout Catholicism. He prayed to the Virgin that she keep his mother alive for the duration of the trip he was about to take so that they might see each other again.

Finally, as he left, he said to Lola, 'This is not my trip. It is my brother's, but I have to make it.'

Perhaps his prayers to the Virgin in his luggage were not in vain, for his mother, though frail, was still there to greet him when he arrived in Bethlehem a few weeks later. He stayed for three months. So grateful was he for the Madonna's apparent intervention that he broke his return journey in France and made a pilgrimage to Lourdes so that he could say his prayers again and give his thanks, as if in person.

And then he made for home. Nobody remembers now how he made the long part of the trip – whether it was by train and by ship, or by plane courtesy, perhaps, of BSAA – but he made it all the same. Certainly by late July 1947 he had arrived in Buenos Aires, just a short plane ride away from a reunion with Lola and their children.

Martha Limpert would have been forgiven if all she felt on arriving back in Buenos Aires was relief. The previous decade had not been kind to her. In the late 1930s her husband, Julius, who was born in Hamburg, announced that he wanted to see Germany one more time before he died. Like so many European immigrants Julius and Martha, who was from Berlin, had made a good life for themselves in Chile. They owned great stretches of fertile land around Temuco, hundreds of miles to the south of Santiago, and the farming there had treated them well. Their children were grown up now and they could afford to make the trip. It seemed the right moment to go, but history was against them. They arrived in Germany in 1939 just in time to be trapped there by the outbreak of war.

There were letters home, once or twice a year, but they came heavily censored and there was never a return address. When the fighting came to an end and chaos engulfed continental Europe, the Limperts found themselves in Germany's British-controlled zone. All they wanted to do now was return to Chile and the comfort of their family but for many months nobody was allowed to go anywhere. The Allies were in the throes of creating the international war crimes tribunal that would sit at Nuremberg. There was great concern that members of the Nazi party who might have to stand trial could escape the country if sufficient investigations were not carried out into each and every applicant. All names would have to be checked against Nazi party records still held in Berlin.

In early 1946 the Allied powers and the governments of South America established the Latin-American Repatriation Scheme. Citizens of countries like Argentina and Chile could finally go home as long as the British gave them an exit permit from their part of Germany and the host country issued them with an entry visa. (It was a smart and rigorous plan on paper although in practice it was deeply flawed. It is estimated that thousands of Nazis, many of them high-ranking army and party officials, escaped to South America after the war.)

Sometime in 1946 the Limperts applied for permission to leave. In January 1947 Julius was given clearance. His name appeared on a list of around three dozen Chileans who the British said had been investigated by MI6, the British foreign intelligence service, and found to have no Nazi connections. Sadly the news came too late for Julius: he died in late February or early March 1947, still in Germany. By then Martha was still waiting for news about her case and was more desperate than ever to get back to

Temuco and her children. Later in March the Chilean ambassador to Britain, Manuel Bianchi, intervened on her behalf. 'Señora Limpert is particularly anxious to leave soon,' he wrote to the British authorities in Germany, 'as her husband has just died and she is now alone aged 70 or so.' She already had her entry visa for Chile, he said, so there was no reason for any delay.

It was not until the next month that her name was advanced to British intelligence for priority clearance. Going through their records they discovered that she had already received it, months before. In a classic bureaucratic confusion she had ended up on the same January list as her husband but under the name Martha Hornisch-Jahre de Limpert. The long, exotic surname is likely to have been a combination of her husband's name and her maiden name. As her husband's full surname was Limpert-Held, she also turned up on another list as Martha Held. And so she became lost in the system: the woman with three names and only one exit visa. She should have been on her way home by early spring at the latest. Instead by May she was still languishing amid the rubble and confusion of post-war Germany.

Once the mistake had been spotted she was finally cleared to leave in July. There was just one last problem, as the Chilean ambassador explained: she had passage aboard a BSAA flight to Santiago leaving London in late July. She would therefore need a transit visa to cover her for one day in London, which normally took four weeks to arrange. Could the British authorities accelerate the issuing of such a visa so she could make her flight? They agreed that they could. The visa arrived in time.

Finally, on 27 July 1947, Martha Limpert left Germany on board a Dutch aircraft. With her she carried an urn containing her husband's ashes. She was going home.

For Paul Simpson the flight from the Argentinian capital which he was preparing to take that August was nothing more than routine. He had taken dozens like it in the preceding years and he had good reason to think he would take dozens more in the years to come. If, that was, he stuck with his job as a diplomatic messenger for King George VI, and it wasn't at all certain that he would. Letters home to his adoring teenage niece Christine, sent the previous year from a rainswept Madrid, suggested a man both hungry for time at home and less than enamoured with the rigours of constant travelling. If you stripped out the travelling, there wasn't much else to the job: a King's Messenger who wanted to stay at home was of no use to anyone.

A corps of messengers working on behalf of the British monarch had existed since 1199. Though the name now looked like an anachronism in an age when the constitutional monarch had no political power, there was still a need for sensitive government material – generally from the Foreign Office, by whom the messengers were employed – to be hand-delivered about the globe. Prior to the outbreak of war the messengers' numbers had fallen to little more than a dozen, with many of their deliveries being undertaken by ships' captains. But with the fall of France in 1940 the British government decided the time had come to expand the corps once again and their ranks swelled to fifty-seven. Most of them were middle-aged ex-military men who were considered too old to be of any use on active service but too young and fit to be dispensed with entirely.

Paul Simpson was different. He had never been in the forces. Instead he joined the Foreign Office from Thomas Cook, the travel company, where his self-taught mastery of multiple languages had made him an expert and reliable organizer of trips for others. Nevertheless he looked the part of the Foreign Office man: he was tall and his prematurely silver-grey hair gave him an air of gravitas well beyond his forty-three years. What's more he was a fabulous tennis player who could take on two opponents at once, Christine boasted to her friends. That sort of thing went down very well with the diplomatic corps, for whom working life all too often comprised long periods of inactivity followed by sudden flurries of intense work. A bit of gamesmanship helped to pass the time. Soon after he joined the civil service Simpson was assigned to the messenger corps and began his travels, stationed at first in Angola and then with the British legation in Montevideo, Uruguay. Within a few months the United States had entered the war and he was moved on to the British embassy in Washington. He began hopping across the country on trips which Christine could follow from the trail of garish, super-tinted postcards he sent back to her. She learnt more, though, from the pictures – of cotton-pickers 'Down in Sunny Dixie' or 'Maxwell Street Chicago' or 'The Old State House, Boston' – than she ever could from the messages her dashing uncle wrote. The censor looked across them all and so dear Uncle

Paul took to composing the blandest of notes imaginable.

His prose might have been dull but his progress was impressive. One card arrived from Chicago dated 8 October 1942 – 4 a.m. It was followed by another, dated later the same day from Omaha, Nebraska. The message read: 'Am now about half way across the United States in the wide open spaces.' And then there was a third on 8 October, this time from Salt Lake City, Utah. (Message: 'Still on the way and feel very thirsty. It must be the salt around here.') The day after that he was in Seattle. ('Arrived here last night. Leave for Vancouver today.') And on 9 October, Vancouver itself. ('Fine city surrounded by sea and mountains.') There were other cards at other times from Jamaica and Haiti, from Puerto Rico and Mexico City and Colombia. There were pictures of pelicans in Louisiana and palm trees in the Caribbean. There was an aerial shot of the mighty Corcovado mountain in Rio with its towering statue of Christ, his arms outstretched. There were exquisite rose arbours in Jacksonville, Florida. There were native Americans from Guatemala in full national dress. To a schoolgirl living through the gloomy days of war back in Surrey it was all improbably glamorous. She treasured each one of these cards and put them away safely to keep.

For Simpson it was almost certainly less thrilling as the job brought with it onerous responsibilities. The title King's Messenger suggested scrolls of vellum tucked carefully into secret jacket pockets or perhaps, to be modern, a black attaché case handcuffed to an official wrist with a solid click. In reality the diplomatic bag was a white canvas sack so large that it needed an aircraft seat to itself and the messenger was never allowed to let it out of his sight, even for a moment. If the plane he was travelling on had to stop over for a short period, the messenger could not get off unless another diplomat from the local embassy or consulate was there at the airport to come on board and sit by the bag. To add to this drudgery, the endless travelling had played a part in the end of his marriage to Betty, his wife of eighteen years from whom he was now separated. He kept in touch with their son Patrick by letter and made sure that his private education was funded, but it was not the same as being there.

When he arrived in Buenos Aires in late July or very early August 1947 he could not even take pleasure in the novelty of the trip. He had been there before, in April 1942. It was, he wrote back to Christine then, 'the most beautiful city in South America'. And now he was preparing to leave it, complete with his diplomatic bag addressed to Jack Leche, Britain's ambassador to Chile in Santiago.

These, then, were the first three passengers who would board the *Star Dust*: the Chilean-Palestinian Casis Said Atalah, the Chilean-German Martha Limpert and the British King's Messenger, Paul Simpson.

CHAPTER NINE

BATHURST WAS A ROUGH PLACE TO FLY FROM. IT WAS A terrible place to crash. At 04.08 on 7 September 1946, nine months after that inaugural BSAA flight to South America which had come so close to ending in the sea, Captain John Cummings took off from the Gambian airfield in *Star Leader*, an Avro York, bound for Natal, Brazil. There were twenty passengers on board. Cummings was an experienced pilot inasmuch as they all were. He'd seen out the war piloting a variety of aircraft but, unlike most of the other boys, the Lancaster bomber had not been one of them. Experience of the old Lancs might have come in handy now with the York. It was, essentially, the same plane. A different body and an extra tailfin up the back, but they were relatively small differences. A little more experience of the York itself might have come in handy too, but there just hadn't been the time. Cummings had had less than four hours' flying time on Yorks during daylight, and his night-time flying amounted to no more than 63 minutes. What's more, *Star Leader* was heavier than any aircraft he had flown before. Ever obsessed by the profit margin, Bennett had argued that the York could easily get off the ground at 72,000 pounds – 4,000 pounds more than it was certified for. Forget what the certificates claim, he said. Certificates were just the paper trail left behind by bureaucrats and everybody knew how much he hated them. If he could prove the weight limits on the certificates were flawed he would be proving that the government men who wrote them were equally useless. He loaded up the test planes so that he could squeeze every last penny out of every flight, and up they went. But that was in the cool temperate air over Heathrow, not the dank, sauna-like conditions of the tropics in which aircraft behave differently. The York that Cummings was piloting that humid, equatorial night-dark morning weighed 68,770 pounds. He had never before flown anything that weighed more than 65,000 pounds and had no experience of how a heavier plane might handle.

Star Leader took off towards the south and climbed steeply before disappearing from view. No one knows what happened next. Did Cummings think all was well until he realized he was not in control of his over-burdened aircraft and that they were climbing too quickly? Did he pull hard on the stick to keep the nose up, willing his crate into the air? Was the truth unavoidable as his thudding York failed to comply with the basic laws of aviation, those hidden calculations that should have kept 68,770 pounds of metal and fuel and cargo and passenger in the air?

The noise of the crash came a few seconds after take-off and then a wretched dull glow lit the night sky. The burning wreckage was found in the bush two miles south of the airfield. All twenty-four passengers and crew were dead. It was the second incident to have befallen BSAA at the airfield in less than ten days. On 30 August a Lancastrian called *Star Glow* had swung off the runway as it speeded along for take-off. It crashed into an unmarked ditch and, while there were no casualties, the aircraft was a complete write-off. They were lucky then but not now; there were twenty-four corpses to be shipped home. For the more superstitious BSAA pilots Bathurst was now clearly jinxed. A bad airfield in a bad country. The company soon moved its African operations to Dakar in Senegal, seventy miles away.

Among the BSAA crews the fatal crash of *Star Leader* was accepted as one of those things, the hand that fate occasionally deals those who fly for a living. The pilots of BSAA were used, during their Pathfinder days, to losing a minimum of ten or twenty aircraft a night and with them all those on board. Wasn't it inevitable that there would still be losses, they said. Aviation carried risks, whether it was military or civilian, and the end of a war didn't change that. The pilots of the rival BOAC would have disagreed but Bennett had gone to great lengths to inculcate his men in a different culture. BOAC was for plodders. BSAA was for heroes.

For some in BSAA, however, the danger signals were there a long way out. One Stargirl had already departed to work for a charter airline, announcing to her colleagues that under Don Bennett 'life is expendable'. She was, she said, determined to hang on to hers. A number of the more cautious pilots were beginning to have their doubts. One day in the early months of operations a pilot called Lincoln Lee was asked by one of Bennett's senior managers whether he would like to do a few flights in a Lancastrian down to Bermuda, which the company was just beginning to serve. A bit of extra flying experience, if he wanted it. Lee pointed out that he'd never flown into Bermuda, nor, for that matter, had he flown a Lancastrian at night, as the route required. He asked if he could do a couple of circuits in one during the hours of darkness just to practise a night-time landing.

'Well, if you feel like that,' his manager said, 'we can always find someone else.' Eventually Lee managed to convince Bennett to let him practise landing in the dark, though it took great persistence.

Cliff Alabaster also had his worries. He had been hired to head the airline's navigation operation, a difficult task given Bennett's presence. The great Bennett would always be his own navigation officer. One morning in 1946 Alabaster was in his office housed in one of the tatty prefabricated huts that ringed the developing airfield out at Heathrow, working on route information for the pilots: local maps for each airport, advised landing patterns, frequencies for the few radio beacons that were available. It was standard stuff, the sort of information that pilots of any civil airline could expect to be issued with. Bennett walked in and saw what he was doing.

'What are those?' he said.

'They're route books,' Alabaster said.

Bennett sniffed. 'You don't need them.' His pilots didn't need their hands held, they could find their own way down. That's how things worked in BSAA.

Alabaster protested in the only way he thought would make sense to Bennett. 'It's not going to cost anything,' he said. Grudgingly the boss let him continue.

A little while later David Brice, the chief pilot, came in to see Alabaster. It was common knowledge that Brice wasn't happy. He thought his job was to fly the airline's aircraft and oversee the pilots. Bennett had loaded him with countless other duties, including planning routes and choosing airfields, tasks which he didn't feel were part of his job.

'It's too much, Alaby,' Brice said. 'I'm leaving.'

'Why?' Alabaster said.

'I can't work for a madman any longer.' Alabaster watched him go. While he might not have chosen the term 'madman' himself – it wasn't his kind of language – he was definitely beginning to agree with the sentiment. Bennett had the potential to be a dangerous man. Brice left BSAA shortly afterwards to return to BOAC where he had previously been employed.

Down in South America the airline was also gaining for itself a truly terrifying reputation. The airport authorities at Rio were becoming increasingly infuriated with some of the pilots who seemed unwilling to take the long approach to the runway when there was cloud overhead. Instead they would turn out to sea and drop down through the cloud base to fly in very low through the harbour mouth, on a few occasions missing the masts of the boats bobbing there on the water by only a few feet. In August of 1946 the British embassy in Rio sent an urgent telegram to the Civil Aviation Ministry in London. 'The real trouble is that the pilots of British South American Airways are continually breaking the regulations,' the diplomat wired. 'There is an almost complete lack of flying discipline for which Air Vice-Marshal Bennett must take certain responsibility. He himself when here had greatly offended the air authorities by a particularly glaring violation of local regulations.' Bennett had taken off without clearance from the controllers because he was tired of waiting.

The British embassy down in Montevideo, capital of Uruguay, didn't like him that much either. Diplomats had spent long hours with the local aviation authorities negotiating arrangements for BSAA which Bennett was merely meant to sign up to. Instead he turned up at the meetings and thumped the table and demanded the right to renegotiate all the terms. 'His efforts were unsuccessful,' reported a British government official later, in the careful language of the civil service, 'and caused some embarrassment to HM Ambassador.'

For the mandarins of Whitehall, however, the real concern was with the much larger country immediately to the south of Uruguay: Argentina. Since the middle of the nineteenth century Argentina had been viewed as an official outpost of Empire; a mighty store of meat and grain for the British people who, in return, would provide the capital necessary to help develop the country's industry and infrastructure. In 1889, the peak year of this informal deal, between 40 and 50 per cent of all British investment overseas poured into Argentina. The result was that the wealthy Anglo-Argentinian community, which expanded throughout the century as people arrived to run the industries set up with British cash, became a part of the ruling elite. In the twentieth century, however, the currents of social politics began to turn against the British as nationalists mounted a concerted effort to 'argentinize' the country. Eventually it led to the rise of the charismatic Juan Domingo Perón, an army officer democratically elected to the presidency in October 1946 after playing a part in the military coup of 1943.

The prevailing and simplistic view of Perón, at least in the British press of the time, had him down as nothing more than a fascist, a close cousin of the jack-booted administrations the Allies had just wasted so many lives and so much time defeating. Certainly he had been a part of the Argentinian government which, to the dismay of the British establishment, had stayed neutral throughout the war. They had expected loyalty at the very least. Instead Argentina had displayed a marked tolerance for the Axis powers. Others saw Perón merely as a nationalist and a populist driven more by anti-American sentiment than anything else. Either way he presented major problems for Britain. On the political–military front there was the question of a small cluster of rocky islands in the South Atlantic known to the British (who held them) as the Falklands and to the Argentinians (who wanted them back) as Las Malvinas. Perón swiftly reasserted his country's sovereignty over them as part of a greater claim to territories in the

Antarctic. In 1947 Britain was even moved to dispatch warships to the area to prove its commitment to the British subjects living there.

On a practical level was the more basic issue of Argentinian meat being supplied to Britain, which was in desperate need of the protein. From 1946 onwards British trade delegations regularly arrived in Buenos Aires to re-negotiate terms for Argentinian beef imports in a series of meetings which were never less than fraught. (In London *The Economist* despaired of the negotiating tactics being used by Perón's men which, the newspaper said, were 'obviously not learnt at a public school'.) The thought that into this mêlée would fly the flippant, tetchy and un-predictable Don Bennett as a representative of British trade would have terrified the sensitive chaps of the Foreign Office. Bennett did have one meeting with Perón, during which he tried to hustle a contract to fly cargo and passengers on behalf of his government. He did not get the business.

Beyond these issues, though, there always stood the most practical worry with BSAA: crashes. In the early hours of 13 April 1947 a BSAA York, *Star Speed*, was heading towards the airfield at Dakar when the pilot received a concerned message on his radio from another BSAA pilot going north. Fog patches were starting to form in the Dakar area, he said. It looked dodgy and he might want to start thinking about an alternative landing strip, perhaps over at Bathurst. There were no radio beacons at Dakar nor, for that matter, any landing lights. Generally pilots identified the airfield by the beams of the lighthouse out on the coast a short distance away. By the time *Star Speed* arrived overhead there was a little less than an hour's fuel in the tanks and the pilot decided that was not enough for a major diversion. For much of the remaining sixty minutes he attempted to find the runway, dipping down towards the ground in the gloom and the fog and then back up again. The controller eventually suggested he try diverting to an airfield at Thies thirty-seven miles away but the pilot didn't have Thies on his maps. In any case as far as he knew there were no landing lights there either. He had no choice, he said. He would have to bring her down at Dakar as close to the runway as possible and hope for the best.

He got the worst. As *Star Speed* landed it hit a pile of rocks and then, further on, crashed into a baobab tree, destroying the aircraft. Of the six crew only two were slightly injured. The rest escaped unhurt. Seven of the nine passengers were killed.

Back in London Bennett was summoned to a meeting at the Civil Aviation Ministry with Peter Masefield, himself a leading aviator and now a civil servant in the department. Masefield raised the question of safety but Bennett batted the enquiry away. He was not about to be given lectures by petty bureaucrats on how to run an airline.

'It's not as bad as it might have been,' he told Masefield bullishly. 'We've done a tremendous lot of flying in pretty bad weather. We've had fewer casualties than we had in the Pathfinders.' Masefield was not impressed. The man was supposed to be running an airline, not Bomber Command.

At Heathrow the camaraderie was still intact despite the problems they were facing. There was even a little gallows humour doing the rounds among some of the crew.

The joke concerned the slogans of the competing airlines and it ran like this:

BOAC will take good care of you.
BEA will get you there and back again.
BSAA will inform your next of kin.

CHAPTER TEN

The Passengers – Part II

ENGLAND WAS A BORE. A WRETCHED, CRUSHING, PITIFUL BORE. Jack Gooderham thought so, and he'd seen enough of the world to know. It was bleak and cold, a country so exhausted by the fight for survival that it didn't know what to do with itself now that it had won. No place for a businessman, certainly not one like Jack with his 'interests' and his 'going concerns' and his 'connections'. No place for a man trying to make his way.

'The trade of the country is going to hell and yet it's impossible to move a hand to better matters,' he wrote to his younger brother Paddy in South Africa, in September of 1945. He knew why, though. It was that 'gang of elderly trades union officials' who were governing the country as part of Clement Attlee's bloody Labour government. It was as if they genuinely didn't want him to do business, what with all the post-war controls and committees put in place to regulate trade. 'I am too old to be communized,' he declared mournfully in another letter to his brother a year later, though he was a young man really, the same age as Paul Simpson, the King's Messenger. Jack would have turned forty-three on 4 August 1947 were it not for a flight from Buenos Aires to Santiago that he took two days before.

Eric John Salt Gooderham was born in 1903 in the Tower of London where his father was a yeoman of the guard. Where the Salt in his name came from no one was absolutely sure. It wasn't a family name. They assumed instead that it came from the Salt Tower at the Tower of London where, like his brother Paddy, he lived and was probably born. It didn't matter much because nobody used the name. They just called him Jack, and always had done. His father, Albert, had been a sergeant major in the Norfolk Regiment until 1896, often fighting overseas and winning medals, and his position at the Tower was a retirement job. There he and his much younger wife Elizabeth could see out their days together with their two young boys, now that the two older children, Robert and Elsie, were off their hands. It is said that dug deep into the wall of the bedroom Jack and Paddy shared within the Tower ramparts are Jack's initials. He carved them there to mark the spot, though no one in the family has seen the graffiti for many years. But Jack wasn't a vandal, or at least his headmaster didn't think so. 'He is gentlemanly in his actions and quite free from boyish frivolity,' the head wrote in a reference for Jack as he moved on to his new school when he was thirteen.

It is a fine reference for a child of his times, if not one that describes the dynamic businessman Gooderham became. It was textiles that made his fortune and by the time war broke out his company, Dreyfuss, was considered such a force in the buying and trading of wool that it was designated a strategic industry, necessary for the war effort. He was never called up. Instead he became wealthy by supplying cloth to the military who needed it for their uniforms. By the mid- to late 1940s he was a man with multiple interests and contacts across the world. As well as Dreyfuss he owned Marine Trading, which dealt in mother-of-pearl shells dredged from the depths of the Red Sea for expensive buttons. There was Argu and Co., which had warm pre-war contacts in the Italian silk business. There was W. Lockwood, which dealt in antique furniture and Oliver & Co., which was looking to move into Irish tweeds when 'the time is ripe'. He knew people in Turkey and Holland, Belgium and France and, if the opportunity came his way, he might start trading in champagne and cherry brandy.

But money brought responsibilities and he attended to those. He kept a big house in Limpsfield, Surrey where his mother Elizabeth lived attended by a housekeeper. He was generous to his family and offered his relations jobs if they needed them. These things he could afford to do, though no amount of wealth could deal with the drudgery and dreariness of English life: the shortages of food and the high cost of new shoes at his shoe makers (£9 and 10 shillings) or the price of a new double-breasted suit in the current loose style (£25). These were prices he could well afford but still, he hated paying them.

'Life here is rather dull at the moment after all the thrills of the past several years,' he wrote in one letter. 'We have not yet got used to not being bombed and it's strange to have leisure again without feeling that one is slacking.' Eventually he buried himself in his work and travelled a lot to Europe where he could indulge his passion for skiing or simply soak up a little uncommon sunlight. He thought of starting a family but it never happened. 'If I had time I might get married but I never have time to concentrate,' he confessed. 'Just as well I imagine as I would make a pretty hopeless spouse.'

Finally he announced to Paddy that he was making plans to live his life elsewhere. He would slog his guts out for the next two years and then move abroad, maybe to Switzerland. 'I have many good friends in Switzerland and run over there fairly often these days and am in love with the country,' he said. 'It's all so clean and pre-war – even smug – and so utterly different and pleasant after this land where everything is in short [supply] and a struggle to come by.' It would make him happy. He had never asked for much from life, he said, 'save decent clothes and food, a glass of wine with my meals and reasonably decent living accommodation'. While he waited to achieve his modest dream he would just have to find his pleasures in the transitory joys of travel.

Harald Pagh loved travel too. Harald loved a lot of things: fly fishing and skiing, parties and the company of beautiful women. Here's a picture of Harald with friends at a party in full black tie, smiling warmly at his companions, a bottle of champagne in the ice bucket before them, cork popped. And here, on the ski slopes, tanned and relaxed, hair slicked back, a cravat tied at the neck. And here again in front of all the aircraft he so loved to fly in. Harald was a man of the world and how better to get about that world than by air?

He was born in Denmark in November 1906 but moved when he was two to the small Slovak town of Lučenec, where his father managed a textile factory. At home with his brother Julius and sister Didi he spoke Danish but at school he was taught in Hungarian until Slovak became the official language in 1918. He lived in an age and in a part of *Mitteleuropa* where languages flowed like rivers across borders one into the other; as well as Danish, Hungarian and Slovak, he was fluent in German and could more than get by in English, French and Italian. It was a facility for languages that would serve him well when he followed his father into the textile business by setting up a wool business called Wollimex. Eventually he settled in Zürich and in the 1940s took Swiss nationality and enjoyed the perks of the country's wartime neutrality. It meant that while Europe was paralysed by the sclerosis of conflict he could still travel. He would make his way to Slovakia and turn up unannounced armed with the fresh fruit and luxuries that his brother and his family or his widowed mother Helga could not get hold of. This was the image that stayed with his little niece Stella: the glamorous uncle, who could bring a little light into a dim world of food shortages and ration cards.

In the summer of 1946 Harald came to Slovakia again,

this time accompanied by a friend he had made through his wool business. His name was Jack Gooderham and together they were travelling through Europe, making contacts, meeting friends, having a gas. Soon they were making plans for the big adventure, a grand trip that both of them so wanted to make to South America. It was a place untainted by war, they were told. Business opportunities were plentiful there. Anyway, Harald had a friend in Santiago whom he had not seen since before the war; it was time to renew old friendships. On 13 or 14 July, Harald and Jack went to see Jack's mother at the house in Limpsfield. 'Harald took a lot of photos of the house and garden and ourselves in it,' Elizabeth later wrote in a letter to Harald's mother, Helga. 'He told us he was making a film and that we would be filmstars. I think he was beginning a record of the trip starting from here.'

On the way down the east coast of South America they stopped in Rio for a couple of days before moving on to Buenos Aires where they arrived on 25 July, the depths of the Argentinian winter. Harald hopped over to Montevideo on the last day of July to meet a few business contacts and later that day he sent a postcard to his niece back in Slovakia. 'Dear little Stella!' he wrote. 'It is terribly cold here now. Warm greetings from your naughty Uncle Harald who writes so little. Kisses!' For a while it seemed Harald and Jack's journey would stop there. For some reason the authorities in Chile did not seem willing to issue them with the visas they needed to make the trip. They made calls to their friend in Santiago and pleaded with the authorities. Eventually the paperwork came through and on 2 August they were ready for the next leg of their trip to Santiago.

Peter Young had visited Santiago many times before. He even met his wife there. Elenor was working for the American embassy in the Chilean capital when they first met in 1939, and he was working as a representative of the British tyre company Dunlop, travelling all over South America. In April 1940 he wrote from São Paulo, Brazil to his mother in England. He was to be married, he said, and her future daughter-in-law was 'a Scotch girl . . . by name Elenor Hampden from the county of Angus'. She was, he said, the same age as he, thirty-four. She had been married once before, was widowed and had a daughter, also called Elenor. A ready-made family, then, for the man who had shown no clear desire to settle down at all.

Like Paul Simpson's family, Peter Young's followed his progress by the postcards that fell like confetti on to their doormat: from Cuernavaca in Mexico and Montevideo in Uruguay and the plush country club in Lima, Peru. There were pictures of the grand monuments to republicanism that the South American states so loved to erect and of the ancient Aztec burial grounds. The image which most sums up his life is a photograph of Peter himself, standing in the Plaza de Mayo, Buenos Aires in 1941. He is wearing an immaculate white double-breasted suit, creases just so, and from beneath the turn-ups of his loose trousers peek a delicious pair of co-respondent shoes, black or brown at the tips, white behind, and dark again about the laces. He clutches in his hands a white Panama hat. But it is his gaze, fixed away out of the frame, which is most striking. It is as if this lean, elegant man is elsewhere, distracted, in search of the next adventure.

Peter Young was born in 1906, the middle child of three, and the only son. During the First World War Young's father, a clergyman, wrote a controversial pamphlet on the role of the church in the war effort. He was probably also a conscientious objector who, like a number of others, preached against the dispatch of Britain's young men to the front where they faced an almost certain death in the pursuit of an uncertain cause. Eventually he resigned from his parish in West Yorkshire and only returned to his calling a few years later when he was invited to become the vicar of a parish in York. Peter's was not a privileged childhood. Nevertheless the money was found to send the beloved son to St Edmund Hall college at Oxford University. On graduating he put his education to good use and, at the same time, indulged his developing passion for travel by becoming tutor to Prince Michael of Romania in Bucharest. It was said he got the job because a great uncle had performed the same task, decades before, to Princess Mary of Teck.

By 1934, and already a high-ranking executive with Dunlop, he was rich enough to give his sister Margaret £100 as a wedding present, a fortune in those days and certainly sufficient to pay for a car. Then it was off to South America and a world untroubled by conflict. He wrote often and worried that his relatives were short on food or safety. To those back in England, it was clear that his was a different kind of life entirely. At Christmas 1946 he proved it when he arrived to visit them accompanied by the gorgeous Elenor, who smelt so good and looked so marvellous in her fox furs and her high heels. They brought chocolates wrapped in silver foil and, for the girls, dolls with working eyes. There was music on a wind-up gramophone and songs and a collapsing opera hat. 'The war-dark house sparkled,' wrote his niece Stacy many years later, 'and as they put on their 78s and danced the Tango, it was better than Fred and Ginger.'

Peter had crossed the Andes before, of course. There was not much in South America he had not done. In February 1942 he wrote from Buenos Aires of 'a three day journey' across the peaks. That, obviously, had been by land. This time, in 1947, the trip back to Santiago would be by air. Elenor would not be with him. She had to stay in Scotland to see her daughter off to boarding school. Her husband would have to make the trip alone.

These then were the last three passengers who would board the *Star Dust*: the English businessman Jack Gooderham, the multilingual wool trader Harald Pagh, now of Switzerland, and the English expatriate Peter Young.

Each of them was somebody's dashing uncle or brother.

CHAPTER ELEVEN

IT WAS CLIFF ALABASTER'S THIRTEENTH TRIP IN COMMAND. IT was the one he would never forget. On 26 January 1947 he took off from London in the Lancastrian *Starlight* bound for Bermuda by way of Santa Maria in the Azores. Halfway into the trip BSAA's senior Stargirl, Joan Thompson, came on to the flight deck.

'One of the passengers has passed out,' she said. It was a Polish woman, a Mrs Kowalska, travelling with her husband.

'What's the husband doing?' Alabaster asked.

'He's up the back smoking,' she said, with a shrug. He didn't look too concerned. Together they agreed it would be best if they carried on to Santa Maria, where there was a BSAA office, rather than turn back for France or Portugal and find an emergency airfield where facilities might be uncertain.

What was actually going on in the passenger cabin behind him would become the subject of great rancour between the airline and at least one of its passengers, though Alabaster never altered his story. 'I was not once asked to turn back,' he said later. Even his greatest critic could not present any evidence to the contrary.

Sitting near Mrs Kowalska that day was a Mr Urquhart, a Foreign Office official bound for Caracas in Venezuela. Later he would be moved to the embassy in Washington DC from where he would rattle off repeated letters to the Civil Aviation Ministry demanding that something be done. He had seen Mrs Kowalska experiencing her fits and her seizures and there was no doubt in his mind: she was in a terrible way. 'The distraught husband, as a matter of fact, was begging all and sundry in broken English, French and German to have the plane go down,' Urquhart wrote. 'As he rightly said it would be dreadful for his wife to be left in that condition for the [remainder of the] flight to the Azores.' Urquhart watched the stewardess running up and down the cabin. He saw the look on her face. The stewardess must have realized something was up, he said. She must have told the pilot when she went in to see him. But, he admitted, he had no idea what had passed between them.

As they arrived over the Azores one of the Lancastrian's four engines gave out and Alabaster was forced to make a three-engine landing. Finally on the ground, Mrs Kowalska was passed over to the care of local doctors at the airport, who gave drugs by injection, but the convulsions continued. She died shortly afterwards.

Immediately Urquhart fired off a telegram to the Foreign Office.

Fellow passengers in British South American Airways service to Azores January 26th deplore circumstances of death of Polish woman. They hope that court of enquiry will decide whether it was not a mistake to continue flying when it was apparently at a stage that Polish woman's life was in danger.

The morning after Mrs Kowalska's death Urquhart set up a desk in the dining room of the hotel where they had all been forced to stay due to the Lancastrian's faulty engine. One by one he began interviewing the passengers. Now he demanded that Alabaster give a statement too. The pilot refused: Urquhart might be a Foreign Office official, he said, but he had no authority over a BSAA pilot. He would explain himself to his managers and his managers only. That day a York was flown in to help them complete the flight but, unlike the Lancastrian, it did not have the range to make it to Bermuda. Instead Alabaster decided to fly back to West Africa, then out to Natal, up to Trinidad, on to Caracas, finally arriving in Jamaica nearly thirty-six hours later. During that time Alabaster took only catnaps, lying down on the ragged mail sacks stored at the back of the cabin.

'It was loyalty of a sort,' he said, looking back on the trip. 'We had passengers on board who wanted to get to South America. I felt I could do it. I felt the crew could do it. It was, I suppose "the mail must get through" mentality.'

Weeks later, in Washington, Urquhart returned to the case of Mrs Kowalska, determined to get some response. 'The affair really stinks,' he declared in a letter, using language uncommon to the Foreign Office, 'and many people, including foreigners, have smelled it.' The doctor at the Azores was incompetent, he said, and as for BSAA, they were simply trying to hush things up. Reviewing the file on the case at the Ministry of Civil Aviation a civil servant later scribbled a note on the detailed memos contained within. 'Another instance of BSAA's "press-on" spirit,' he wrote. It was not at all clear whether he meant it admiringly. The government concluded it was a matter for the management of BSAA. The airline concluded that Mr Urquhart was a tiresome little bureaucrat who could safely be ignored. Alabaster was exonerated of all blame for Mrs Kowalska's death. The cause of death was given as tuberculosis of the lungs and heart failure.

A few weeks after returning from his chaotic thirteenth command Alabaster received a visitor at Heathrow's hut 43, which he was using as his office. The caller was a Detective Sergeant Holder from Scotland Yard. The police officer wanted to know about Mr and Mrs Kowalska and Alabaster told him all he could, which was not much. DS Holder took his notes. They were, he said, investigating Mr Kowalski (the male form of Kowalska) in connection with the death. A year or so before he had taken a previous wife on board an aircraft. She too suffered from tuberculosis as a result of incarceration in a camp during the war. As the aircraft reached high altitude her damaged lungs gave out and she suffered oxygen deprivation leading to fits and seizures. Shortly afterwards she died and Mr Kowalski collected on generous life insurance. And now here he was again with another tubercular wife aboard another flight which killed her. Their enquiries were continuing but it certainly looked deeply suspicious. Perhaps our Mr Kowalski was specifically finding sick women whom he could later collect upon, the officer said. DS Holder never returned to hut 43, however, and Cliff Alabaster heard nothing more about the case.

Down in Dakar, beneath a burning African sun, there was another corpse that was causing BSAA more than a little local difficulty. Among the dead in the *Star Speed* crash of April 1947 was a young Portuguese man called Fernando de Sousa Costa Pinheiro. He was the son of a wealthy and eminent lawyer from Lisbon. Almost two months after the crash his body was still in Dakar, boxed but unburied. BSAA had tried to bring it back, they told the Foreign Office, but the coffin had been too big to fit into one of their aircraft. There was space for the coffins containing the two children who died in the crash. As for the bigger adult bodies, they were proving troublesome. In the diplomatic and political circles of Lisbon, of which the Costa Pinheiro family was a firm part, BSAA was now being dismissed as a desperate shambles. 'This incident aroused much hostility to BSAA in Lisbon,' wrote the hapless embassy official who had to deal with it. 'It seems to have been felt that BSAA might well have chartered a special aircraft to bring the body home.' BSAA disagreed. Their job was to transport the living, not the dead. They would bring home the corpse, but only when they were ready to do so.

Now the Portuguese press let rip. 'Whose is the moral and material responsibility for the disaster?' thundered an editorial in the *Jornal de Noticias*. 'Emphatically the company's. The company was not the victim of a fortuitous accident. The accident was the result of the pilot's incompetence. In [the] face of the impossibility of landing at Dakar there are other aerodromes less than an hour's flight away at which a landing could have been made without difficulty.' It was all the fault of BSAA and, by association, Bennett. Under this increasing barrage the air vice-marshal now displayed his impressive talent for diplomacy, honed during the cut and thrust of war. He went on the offensive. 'If the relatives concerned continue with their ridiculous and disgusting behaviour we shall not undertake to deliver the body to Lisbon,' he wrote to the Civil Aviation Ministry, 'but will leave it in Dakar.' The ministry decided not to pass on that particular letter. At the end of the summer of 1947 the body of Fernando de Sousa Costa Pinheiro was finally returned to Lisbon for burial – by ship.

Far over on the other side of the world in that late spring and early summer of 1947 another British diplomat was raising his own concerns about the increasingly ramshackle operations of BSAA. Jack Leche was Britain's ambassador to Chile and a man with as little affection for euphemism as Bennett. In early June his air attaché took a BSAA flight from Buenos Aires to Santiago. He was so disturbed about the way the service unfolded that he decided to inform the ambassador. Leche now wrote to Mr Freese-Pennefather of the Foreign Office in London. The letter was marked 'Personal and Confidential' and began, 'More and more complaints keep rolling in . . .' BSAA, he said, was so against excess expenditure that its aircraft took on only enough fuel to get them direct to Santiago. There was none in the tanks to cope with delays caused by bad weather. On his attaché's trip the flight had run into a brutal front and there was simply not enough fuel to get them to Santiago or back to Buenos Aires. Instead, practically flying on vapour, they diverted to Mendoza. 'But the corporation had made no arrangements for obtaining fuel from Intava, the only organization operating on the airfield there,' Leche wrote. 'Matters were not made easier by the fact that no single member of the aircrew knew a word of Spanish and none of them had been provided with any Argentine currency.' It was left to the air attaché to sort them out. Otherwise the pilot would have been forced to turn to the passengers and beg them to empty their wallets so they could fill up. It was, Leche said, no way to run an airline. 'It reminds me very much of the old story about Cunard [the shipping firm] which was always said to admit that the food was filthy, the service vile etc., but they had never lost a passenger – and this is not good enough.' The Cunard analogy was clearly apt, save in one regard: BSAA had already lost twenty-seven passengers.

Days later Leche was again writing to the Foreign Office about BSAA. This letter was marked 'Secret and Important'. 'I am fully aware that I am making myself a nuisance on this subject,' he now wrote, 'and if this communication is in the form of an official despatch rather than a private letter it is because the position seems to be very serious.'

Leche had been talking to one of BSAA's pilots, a fine and upstanding man whose identity had to remain a secret. He had a family who depended on his income and his job might be put in peril by the intelligence he had passed on if the company ever found out. This pilot was operating services that flew out across to the Caribbean then over to Panama and finally down the west coast of South America, following the spine of the Andes through Lima to Santiago. Down to Panama the weather forecasting was generally excellent. From Panama south, however, the pilot was required to navigate 'by guess and by god', Leche reported. According to this man, Leche went on, 'sooner or later we should lose an aircraft'. All the good weather forecasts came from Pan American Airways and Panagra, BSAA's two North American competitors on what were becoming fiercely fought-over routes. Ever obsessed with making a profit, Bennett was not prepared to pay over the odds for their forecasts. 'In many cases [the BSAA pilot] and his brother captains were able to obtain meteorological reports privately from individual members of Pan American Airways out of pure friendship,' Leche said. 'But that is not the way to run an airline.'

He declared that something had to be done. 'Not only is British prestige involved,' Leche concluded, 'but also the lives of crews and passengers.'

The crew of BSAA's service CS – for Chile, southbound – number 59, departing Heathrow 29 July 1947, might well have been interested in the things His Majesty's ambassador to Chile had to say about the airline for which they worked. But none of this would be made available to the public for decades; that was how the British Foreign Office liked to treat letters marked 'Secret and Important'. By then, of course, the crew of CS59 would be long gone.

CHAPTER TWELVE

Argentina

1999

ATILIO BALDINI LAUGHED WHEN HIS FRIEND GUSTAVO MARÓN told him. He didn't care what José Moiso had said. The *Star Dust* couldn't be up in the mountains. It was at the bottom of the Pacific, or had been, once, before the salt water had dissolved it away to nothing. He was sure of it. The Lancastrian had gone straight over the top, bashed through low cloud and ditched into the sea. That was why no wreckage had ever been found. If it had crashed into the mountains somebody would have found something by now. Nothing could stay hidden like that for half a century, not even on those brutal wind-blown peaks.

Whatever Baldini said, José was certain of his information. True, some of Pablo Reguera's account was a little odd. When Reguera and José first spoke about the find, Reguera stated emphatically that the engine he saw on Tupungato was a small one, just a few feet across. A small engine would not be powerful enough to get an aircraft to a site 4,500 metres up a mountainside where it apparently crashed, let alone above the 7,000 metres needed to clear the Andes. It was probably a confusion, brought on by the low oxygen atmosphere at altitude. Oxygen deprivation can affect anybody, even an experienced climber like Reguera. Doubt was certainly not a good reason to delay an expedition and time was now of the essence. Usually José and his son Alejo would start planning a trip to a mountain as uncompromising as Tupungato in the very depths of winter in order to be ready to go the moment the weather changed. But it was already late November, the heart of the Argentinian spring, and the hot smell of summer was in the air.

In January 1999 José went to see Lieutenant Colonel Ricardo Bustos, commander of the Eleventh Mountain Regiment, a solid career soldier of the old school with a harsh crop of grey hair, sharp blue eyes and a tight staccato drumbeat of a voice. If the Moisos were going to make it to Tupungato in time they were going to need the army's help. The father-and-son team might be able to do it without the military, but with them their chances of success would be that much greater. They could supply extra manpower and the pack mules that would be needed to carry all the equip- ment to the lowest base camp. José had already started talking to Sergeant Cardozo, engaging him in long con- versations about viable routes and best approaches and search strategies. Sergeant Cardozo would be a welcome addition to any expedition party; for this assault on Tupungato he was all but a necessity. What's more his enthusiasm would help greatly to encourage the army command.

Bustos took some convincing. It would be a complicated expedition, rife with hazards. He would be sending one of his very best mountain men up in search of relics. That said, it was a job to which Sergeant Cardozo was ideally suited. No one knew Tupungato better than him, and it could bring honour upon the regiment. Lieutenant Colonel Bustos gave the go-ahead; the moment enough additional mules arrived at the army base to replace those that the expedition would take with them, they could go. José agreed. It seemed a reasonable enough condition. He had not bargained for the delay: week after week he waited by the phone in Mendoza for the call that would tell him the mules had arrived and his one attempt at a truly remarkable act could begin. He watched the weather and the shortening days as the burning heat of the Argentinian summer gave way to the first cool breaths of autumn, and began to fear that the opportunity was slipping away from him. Eventually, after almost two months of waiting, the army announced that the mules had been delivered. On 10 March 1999 the Moisos began their expedition to Tupungato, together with Sergeant Cardozo, two other soldiers in support and their various pack mules.

It took a day and a half to reach the site they had identified for their base camp, which lay at an altitude of 2,000 metres. It was tucked in below the formidable – and rarely conquered – south-eastern face. Above them towered another 5,000 metres of rock and ice where they knew the landscape to be creased and curved in on itself. Anything that happened to be scattered about the moraine would be hidden from view; the only way to see what was there was to get as close as possible. The team identified three separate segments of the mountainside to explore, each stretching upwards to the summit. For two days they trudged across them, searching for anything on the slopes ahead that might be man-made and yet not part of the debris left behind by climbers; something sharp and metallic that could announce itself by catching the sunlight and throwing it back at them. All they found was what everybody else always found on Tupungato: endless rock and ice.

There was just one more segment of the mountain to explore but it was not to be theirs. At the end of that second day a ferocious ice storm swept down over the peaks, whipping up the snow from above and cutting off the routes. They would not be going anywhere, either up or down, while the storm was raging. For thirty-six hours they stayed at base camp sheltering in their two tents, the Moisos and Sergeant Cardozo together in one, the two soldiers in the other. They talked of mountains and of climbs or switched on the radio to search for signals from the outside world. Sometimes they just listened to the wind as it blew itself hoarse about them. Moiso knew full well what that sharp keening rush of air meant: their expedition was over, at least for this year.

Sergeant Cardozo had experienced enough of these storms to know just how dangerous they could be. You did not try to second-guess them. Andean storms could be as capricious and untrustworthy as a hormonal adolescent, calm one moment, a raging fury of snow and ice the next. The moment the storm broke, he said, they should get swiftly off the mountain. Nobody disagreed. A plane wreck, whether it was pregnant with gold or not, was an enticing prospect but not worth losing a life over. Seven days after setting off they arrived back at the mountain station, tired and despondent. The expedition had ended in total failure. José could not hide his disappointment. From here on in, as the seasons changed, the weather was only likely to get worse. Tupungato would no longer be merely dangerous, it would become a truly efficient death-trap. What's more, it would be shaped and changed by the weather. A wind storm was bad enough: it shifted the snow about and changed the look of the landscape. But its effect was minimal compared to what snow storms could do. They don't just alter the landscape, they alter the mountain itself, create heavy slopes of ice where before there were none and fill in chasms and gullies so they might as well never have existed. If there was wreckage to be found on Tupungato – and José was still convinced it was there – another heavy winter could hide it away for decades. They might just have lost their only real chance of finding the wreck and José knew it.

That winter was frustrating for the Moisos. Each hint of a blizzard in the mountains sent them rushing for the latest satellite pictures in an attempt to gauge just how deep the snow now lay on the slopes, though it was no substitute for being there. As the year passed José began to wonder if this was as far as they would ever get. The army, which had seemed genuinely convinced that the Moisos were on to something, now appeared to have lost faith. They claimed they didn't have the material resources to spare, that there were not enough mules to lend out for such a trip. To a certain extent José knew it was true: the military was always short on equipment and resources in Argentina. Nevertheless he was sure that if they wanted the climb to go ahead, if they thought it was worthwhile, they could make it happen. José turned on all the charm he used as a salesman of electrical goods, trying very hard to close the deal, but he didn't seem to be getting anywhere.

In January 2000, the height of the summer, José telephoned Sergeant Cardozo. He told him he had had enough of waiting. Time was short. He was going to start the expedition without the mules. At first the soldier tried to talk him out of it but it soon became clear that José's mind was made up. It was as if this was something he not only wanted to do but *had* to do. Sergeant Cardozo stopped fighting. If José was prepared to climb Tupungato without mules then he would go too.

They were saved from what would have been an effort doomed to almost certain failure by a stroke of luck. Each year the army mounts an expedition across the mountains in memory of José de San Martín, the great South American military leader. In the early nineteenth century San Martín led his forces across the Andes to push the Spanish royalists from Chile. The expedition replicates his achievement, although not just with soldiers. Many of the participants are members of the public who pay for the privilege. This year a number had not been able to participate and the army had been left with surplus equipment and pack animals for an Andean climb. With Sergeant Cardozo now pressing for the Moisos' second Tupungato expedition to go ahead, and the materials to do the job available, the top brass finally gave way. At the beginning of the third week of January 2000, the team arrived once more at base camp, ready to restart the search for the *Star Dust*.

CHAPTER THIRTEEN

The Crew

NINA BRAUER-WALTON LIKED THE YOUNG MAN. HE WAS QUIET, but when he did speak he displayed a lovely dry sense of humour. And, of course, he was a flyer, which carried its own particular glamour. Not a flyer like during the war, when members of air crews lived uneasily on borrowed time. This was something far more encouraging. Don Checklin was a pilot with British South American Airways, servicing routes right the way down to Santiago of all places.

She had come across Don often. She met him first through her cousin Moyra who was a member of the Little French Club on St James's Place, just around the corner from London's Piccadilly. Nina loved the Little French Club. It opened in the war, in the narrow Georgian house where Chopin once lived. It was a place where the free French could meet and drink and eat. Now the war was done with and most of the French members had gone. The people who went there these days to down the cheap wine were in the theatre or the film business; young people at the start of exciting careers in a country rediscovering itself. Nina was there because Moyra was her cousin and Moyra was there because her husband, Charlie, was a documentary film-maker. Don Checklin was there because he was close pals with Charlie's brother, the actor Bobby de la Tour: famous Bobby, the first man on to the beaches on D-day; glamorous Bobby, the one the girls wanted to know. There was even an edition of the *Picture Post* which had Bobby on the cover, naming him as a hero just for getting there first. You could be a little bit glamorous simply by standing close to Bobby and warming your hands on the glow of his charisma as he lit up the room. Don was close enough to soak up more than his fair share.

What would they have made of it all back in Derbyshire, home to the lad they knew only as Donald? Glamorous drinking clubs in St James's did not figure hugely in the life of the Checklins. Donald was born in May 1920, the first son of a Methodist minister called George and a Scottish nurse called Mary. His parents met during the First World War while both of them were ministering to the troops in their own ways. Both would continue with their professions; for much of her life Donald's mother was known as Nurse Checklin by more people than knew her as Mary. When he was three the family moved to Gorleston in Derbyshire, not far from the part of northern England where the large Checklin family originally hailed from, but the marriage did not flourish. His parents separated soon afterwards and he and his younger bother – also called George – were left to fight it out for the affections of their formidable mother. Later George would conclude it was a battle Donald had won, though he didn't hold him any ill-will. They were very close as brothers and did almost everything together. They went to boarding school together in Harrogate and together moved on to Nottingham University. Together they owned a Morgan sports car with a lovely long bonnet and an open top. They would cram their gangly long legs into it and speed about the country-side, happy as anything. They were close to their many cousins too but, nobody would deny, clearly different from them. George and Donald spoke with lots of big rounded vowels, unlike the rest of the family who had tight Derbyshire accents. That was what George Senior and Mary had wanted for their sons: a bit of something to set them apart.

George was a scientist. It was his calling. As a child nothing made George happier than the fossils given to him by his uncle Elijah who would dig them up from the coal pit where he was a miner. Donald had other ambitions, though, and in 1940 he joined the RAF. He trained in the USA and then in May 1942 returned to Britain, initially to fly Lancaster bombers. He reached the rank of flight lieu-tenant, served terms with the advanced flying unit and did stints at the various air force training schools. He even won himself a medal. On the night of 14 October 1944, while serving with 158 Squadron, he was dispatched to bomb the German city of Duisburg. As they arrived over the target area for the bombing run the German anti-aircraft guns opened up. The wireless operator was wounded and one of the engines of the Halifax Donald was commanding was seriously damaged. Even so he dropped his bombs and only then made for home. On the return flight the shattered engine finally pulled itself away, ripping a gaping hole in the fuselage. Nevertheless Donald managed to pilot the air-craft back to base in Yorkshire. 'Throughout this incident this captain of aircraft displayed coolness and courage,' the medal citation said, 'and inspired his crew by his determin-ation to overcome all obstacles.' He was awarded a Distinguished Flying Cross and a write-up in his local Derbyshire newspaper, complete with a photograph. It shows a sheepish – perhaps just embarrassed – Donald peering out through the frayed edges of the gouge left by the engine's impact.

As the war came to a close he was posted to special services, flying VIPs about in Lancastrians. It made him an ideal recruit to Don Bennett's new airline. In 1946, his father long dead, he rushed up to Derbyshire to tell the rest of his family about his fine new career.

'I hope it's not a fly-by-night operation,' said his uncle Elijah.

His nephew reassured him. BSAA was a serious outfit, run by a serious man. He was lucky to have the job. He found somewhere to live in Hayes, not far from Heathrow, and began running with the set at the Little French Club.

Sometime in July 1947 Don Checklin asked Nina Brauer-Walton if she would like to have dinner with him. She said yes. They went to a small Greek restaurant on Wigmore Street and drank wine and Don enthused about the trip he was to take the very next day: as second officer aboard BSAA's next service to Santiago. It was his fourth time on the trans-Andean route but each one was something special. It was such marvellous work, he said.

Later, when they were walking through the twilight of a summer's evening, Don pulled Nina into a doorway and kissed her. He said he would call her the moment he returned from Chile in two weeks' time, and she rather hoped he meant it. Perhaps they would go out for another evening. Perhaps he would pull her into another doorway. He was twenty-seven years old.

Hilton Cook had already seen a lot of the world by July 1947, but he had never seen the Andes. At last he would be able to chalk that one up on the slate too: he was rostered to fly as first officer aboard CS59, his first BSAA service all the way down to Santiago. As it happened he had all the pilot licences required to give him full command of the flight but it made sense that he was only first officer on this occasion. He could get a feel for the route, learn its twists and turns. There would always be another opportunity to take the top job.

South America was a long way from where Hilton had begun amid the soot and grime of Stoke Newington, the solid, working-class district of north London where he was born in 1916. His grandfather was a printer and his father an insurance salesman, which put his family a notch above many of their neighbours, mired in city poverty. By the standards of the day they were trade, on more than just nodding terms with the middle classes, and when war broke out for a second time his parents, Laura and Will, swiftly made good their escape. They moved out to the fresher air of Cambridgeshire to avoid the falling bombs. By then Hilton was long gone. He joined the RAF in February 1939, months before the declaration of war, and was soon travelling the country learning to fly Wellingtons. In his spare time he drove his Rover sports car or boxed in amateur fixtures. He was a convincing fighter, they said, a large, well-built man, who won his matches and scored a few knock-outs.

In 1942 he was dispatched to southern Africa, travelling down by sea aboard the *SS Tamaroa*. On 13 April he was presented with a certificate marking his first crossing of the equator. A week later, still out at sea, he received another certificate, this time for a rather less passive achievement. He had, according to the citation, won his 'Novice Heavyweight Semi-Final, held in accordance with the inter-service boxing regulations'. On arrival he was posted first to Rhodesia and later to various parts of East Africa. Photographs from the time show a man clearly enjoying his war: toned and tanned beneath an African sun, he sits among his fellow flyers, face wreathed in a big grin. To his family this appetite for military life with its dangers and its larks made sense: they had him down as the boisterous one, much noisier than his older brother Geoff. Hilton was out-going and brave. Some might even say foolhardy. Hilton Cook took life by the scruff of the neck and shook the hell out of it.

He remained in Africa through to the end of the war before returning to Britain and a job with BSAA late in

1945. Aged thirty, he would be the oldest member of the Santiago-bound crew.

Listed to work the radio set for the trip was Denis Harmer, a former public-school boy with an impressive reputation as a cricketer. He joined the army in 1940 before transferring to the RAF where he served as a ground-based radio operator for three years. He joined BSAA in November 1946 and had crossed the Andes six times prior to July 1947. He was twenty-seven years old.

The Stargirl was Iris Evans from Wembley in north-west London, who had served five years during the war as a chief petty officer in the Women's Royal Navy Service. She joined BSAA in February 1947 but, like Hilton Cook, had never before crossed the Andes. She was twenty-six years old.

If the licence had arrived just a few days later Reginald Cook wouldn't have made it. The rotas would have been drawn up and the jobs handed out and the prize simply wouldn't have been his. Bennett would have put someone else in command of service CS59 to Santiago. The boss had his rules: no pilots could take command until they had their first-class navigator's licence. He didn't care how many hours they had in the air. He didn't care what medals were pinned to their chest. His chaps had to know where the hell they were going. Reginald's licence was finally issued on 24 July 1947 just five days before the flight was due to depart. It was also a full two months after Hilton Cook had received his, but that was irrelevant. It didn't matter that

Hilton was, on paper, the more experienced pilot with 2,129 hours on his log book to Reginald's 1,971. Reginald had already done the trans-Andean route a full eight times as first officer. He would take the top seat.

Reginald's family may have been impressed by his achievements but they wouldn't have been surprised. He was a determined man, always had been, even as a lad growing up in Derbyshire (not that far from Donald Checklin). If he made up his mind to do something, he did it – and the thing he was going to do was fly. In 1936, still just eighteen, he joined the Royal Air Force volunteer reserves out at Burnaston airport near Derby. When war came he was quickly mobilized into the RAF proper to train as a navigator. He started on Wellingtons, flying out of an airfield based at Newmarket racecourse, and then went to Wyton in Cambridgeshire, where Bennett would later establish the Pathfinders' HQ. He nearly lost his life there. One night, as he was setting off on a mission, his aircraft crashed on take-off with both a full bomb load and full fuel tanks. It exploded just after impact, but he and the rest of the crew somehow managed to roll away from the blast and the wreckage. They escaped without injury.

Soon he was off to Calgary in Canada to train as a pilot. When he returned in 1944 he decided the time had come to lay down a few roots. He married Cicely Parker, a local girl from Derbyshire whom he'd known for years. Two months later he took up his last RAF posting, flying Mosquito bombers over Germany in 608 Squadron, commanded by Cliff Alabaster, which was part of the Pathfinder group. His was, by all accounts, official or otherwise, an impressive war. He even had a chest full of metalwork and ribbons to prove it: he was awarded the Distinguished Service Order, the Distinguished Flying Cross and the Distinguished Flying Medal. The citations and gushing praise from on high marked him out and when the war came to an end Don Bennett snapped him up. Reginald Cook was exactly the kind of brave fellow he needed for his new airline.

By the summer of 1947 he had clocked up over a dozen full round trips on all the BSAA routes and had even brought back a few trophies. One of them was a watch bought in one of the shiny boutiques of South America. Back in Derbyshire the watch was a symbol of all that was glamorous about Reginald's life. No one spent £40 on something just to tell the time, not in bleak post-war Britain, and certainly not a grammar school boy from Derbyshire. But Reginald did. Reginald lived that kind of life.

Although the licence wasn't officially issued until 24 July he had passed the all-important navigator's exams a week earlier on 17 July. Bennett decided his pilot was clearly competent enough, even if he didn't yet have the piece of paper to prove it. He was given his first command, though one without passengers. BSAA had won a contract to help develop in-flight refuelling systems. Reginald was ordered to fly out to the Azores and dock with a tanker plane which would meet him there in mid-air. Bennett had done the first run. Alabaster had done the second. Now it was Cook's turn. The trip went off without a hitch. Reginald Cook had proved himself. He was twenty-nine years old.

Shortly before he left Reginald made a promise to his brother-in-law, John Parker. He would buy him a watch, he said, one just like the expensive timepiece ticking away on his own wrist. Then he could carry a piece of South America about with him wherever he went.

The five-strong crew of the *Star Dust*, none of them older than thirty, each of them with years of military experience, was ready for duty.

CHAPTER FOURTEEN

SOMETIME LATE IN JULY 1947 CASIS SAID ATALAH TELEPHONED his wife Lola from Buenos Aires. He wanted her to join him for a few days in Argentina. He wanted her to bring their seven-year-old son Nazir along too, so he could see this great city with its broad boulevards and imposing squares. Casis had made reservations for all three of them on a return flight, leaving Buenos Aires on 2 August, the same date as his daughter Maria's first birthday. They would all get home in time to celebrate and what a celebration it would be: the family, together again, after so many months apart. At first Lola went along with the idea. She began arranging the visas they would need to make the trip. She too thought it would be good for Nazir to see a little of the world. But by the time Casis telephoned again she had undergone a change of heart. She had the business to run and there were all the children to look after. There was just too much to do. She couldn't simply expect someone else to take over while she dropped everything to fly across the mountains, however desperate she was to see her husband.

'It's all right,' Casis told her, reassuringly. 'It isn't important. We can do it another time.'

He telephoned once more after that and, as their conversation was coming to an end, he said, 'I am so close to you and yet so far at the same time.' After so many months abroad, on a journey that had taken him halfway around the world and back again, he was now at least on the same continent as his wife. And yet, by land, it would take three full days to cross from the capital of Argentina to the capital of Chile. It made far more sense to fly. Casis was a wealthy man. He could afford it. He had a diamond stitched into the lining of his suit.

It is certain that Casis did not get to Buenos Aires courtesy of the same BSAA service which was due to take him to Santiago. He arrived in the city almost a week before CS59. Likewise, it is known that Jack Gooderham and Harald Pagh were also already in the Argentine capital, meeting contacts, doing business, playing a little golf. The only passenger who definitely did arrive there on CS59 was Martha Limpert, who boarded in London after her Dutch flight from Germany. Who else was on the flight is not known. No details remain of those who originally boarded it in London on the morning of 29 July. Records tend only to be kept of flights that don't make it to their destination, not of the ones that do. Of the route taken to Argentina by the other two passengers – Paul Simpson and Peter Young – no trace remains and while it is possible both of them boarded the service in London it is most likely that the only one scheduled to do the entire trip was Simpson, the King's Messenger. If he did start from London, alongside Martha, there would have been space aplenty in the cabin for many other passengers to keep both him and his big diplomatic canvas bag company. Up to Argentina the route was flown not by a thirteen-seat Lancastrian but by an Avro York which could seat twenty-one.

The very first BSAA flight to Santiago, on 22 April 1946, had been undertaken in its entirety by a Lancastrian. It was called *Star Land* and was commanded by Don Bennett himself; in customary style Bennett decided to do without the night stop in Brazil that would become a standard part of the route. Instead he flew down to Buenos Aires in one go, stopping only to refuel, in a trip that took twenty-four hours without anything as wasteful as sleep or a change of crew. Soon after that first flight, however, the company decided that the Lancastrian would only be used for the high altitude trans-Andean route to which it was better suited. One of the aircraft was duly stationed in South America specifically for the purpose.

Any passengers travelling from London on CS59 would not have been required to travel out to Heathrow under their own steam. BSAA wanted their customers to start their journey in style, perhaps because there was so little of it once they boarded the aircraft, and they collected them in a coach from the Dorchester Hotel on London's Park Lane. It may have been a glamorous start but it was not a leisurely one. Passengers would have been expected at the Dorchester for not much after 07.00 for the journey out to

Air Vice-Marshal Don Bennett, Chief Executive of BSAA, waving from the cockpit of one of the airline's Lancastrians. *Courtesy of the Bennett family*

BRITISH SOUTH AMERICAN AIRWAYS
LONDON–BERMUDA · NON STOP
FLIGHT REFUELLED SERVICE

BSAA Lancastrian Star Dust being prepared for service at Carrasco Airport

SOUTH AMERICAN SCHEDULE
"FLY WITH THE STARS"

STATION		SERVICE BS		SERVICE CS		SERVICE AS	
		GMT	Local	GM	Local	GMT	Local
London	dep.	Sat. 09.25	Sat. 11.25	Wed. 09.25	Wed. 11.25	Tues. & Fri. 09.25	Tues. & Fri. 11.25
Lisbon	arr.	14.35	15.35	14.35	15.35	14.35	15.35
	dep.	15.20	16.20	15.20	16.20	15.20	16.20
Dakar	arr.	Sun. 00.03	Sun. 00.03	Thur. 00.03	Thur. 00.03	Wed. & Sat. 00.03	Wed. & Sat. 00.03
	dep.	00.55	00.55	00.55	00.55	00.55	00.55
Natal	arr.	10.03	07.03	10.03	07.03	10.03	07.03
	dep.	10.55	07.55	10.55	07.55	10.55	07.55
Rio de Janeiro	arr.	17.28	14.28	17.28 Overnight Stop Fri. 12.00	14.28 Overnight Stop Fri. 09.00	17.28 Overnight Stop Thur. & Sun. 12.00	14.28 Overnight Stop Thur. & Sun. 09.00
	dep.	—	—				
Montevideo	arr.			17.49	14.49	—	—
	dep.			18.40	15.40	—	—
Buenos Aires	arr.			19.52 Overnight Stop Sat. 13.55	16.52 Overnight Stop Sat. 10.55	18.17	15.17
	dep.			→		19.00	16.00
Montevideo	arr.			—	—	20.04	17.04
Santiago	arr.			18.22	14.22	—	—

NOTE :
AS – Argentine South Bound
BS – Brazilian South Bound
CS – Chilean South Bound

STATION		SERVICE BN		SERVICE CN		SERVICE AN	
		GMT	Local	GMT	Local	GMT	Local
Santiago	dep.	—	—	Thur. 14.55	Thur. 10.55	—	—
Montevideo	dep.	—	—	—	—	Sat. & Tues. 11.00	Sat. & Tues. 08.00
Buenos Aires	arr.	—	—	18.37	15.27	12.02	09.02
	dep.	—	—	18.55	15.55	13.00	10.00
Montevideo	arr.	—	—	19.59 Overnight Stop Fri.	16.59 Overnight Stop Fri.	—	—
	dep.			11.55	08.55	—	—
Rio de Janeiro	arr.	—	—	17.38	14.38	19.03	16.03
	dep.	Wed. 13.15	Wed. 10.15	18.20	15.20	19.45	16.45
Natal	arr.	19.58	16.58	01.03* Overnight Stop Sat.	22.03 Overnight Stop Sat.	Sun. & Wed. 02.28	Sun. & Wed 23.28†
	dep.	20.35	17.35	12.25	09.25	12.25	09.25
Dakar	arr.	Thurs. 06.28	Thurs. 06.28	22.18	22.18	22.18	22.18
	dep.	07.20	07.20	23.05	23.05	23.05	23.05
Lisbon	arr.	15.58	16.58	Sun. 07.43 Overnight Stop Fri.	Sun. 08.43 Overnight Stop Fri.	Mon. & Thur 07.43	Mon. & Thur 08.43
	dep.	08.25	09.25	08.25	09.25	08.25	09.25
London	arr.	13.34	15.34	13.34	15.34	13.34	15.34

· 01.03 GMT Saturdays   † 23.28 Local Time Tuesdays and Saturdays

NOTE :
AN – Argentine North Bound
BN – Brazilian North Bound
CN – Chilean North Bound

SAFETY-SPEED-SERVICE

MAIN IMAGE: BSAA's Star Land bearing the distinctive starman logo. Star Land was BSAA's first Lancastrian to undertake the entire flight from London to Santiago. Courtesy of Capt. Frank Taylor

LEFT: South American Schedule 'Fly with the Stars'.

RIGHT: AVM Don Bennett.
Courtesy of the Bennett family

LEFT: Reginald Cook, DSO, DFC, DFM, and commander on flight CS59, the ill-fated journey during which Star Dust *went down.*
Courtesy of John Parker

RIGHT: Hilton Cook, first officer aboard flight CS59.
Courtesy of Christopher Cook

FAR RIGHT: Don Checklin, second officer aboard flight CS59.
Courtesy of Patti Holmes

BRITISH SOUTH AMERICAN AIRWAYS

Telegrams: AIRLINES, NATAL
Telephone: 1983

PARNAMIRIM AIRFIELD
NATAL — BRAZIL

BRITISH SOUTH AMERICAN AIRWAYS
PARA QUALQUER PARTE DO MUNDO

BRITISH
SOUTH AMERICAN
AIRWAYS

SOUTH AMERICAN
SCHEDULE

B·S·A·A

VALID FROM
JULY 1947
until further notice

FLY BRITISH

NAME

Form No. 1600

BRITISH SOUTH AMERICAN AIRWAYS

CREW

the airport. After the completion of a few bureaucratic formalities in the simple huts that ringed the airfield, the passengers boarded the Avro York, registration G–AHFD, named *Star Mist*, ready for take-off at 09.25. As well as the passengers there was also a little cargo; BSAA carried all the post destined for South America from Britain.

A short time before take-off Reginald Cook, preparing for his first command, was briefed on his route. He was told that if the weather was not clear over the Andes west of Mendoza he was to take another route, either an arc to the south of the highest peaks crossing via Planchón or north via San Juan, although he would have known all about those alternatives already. After all, this was his ninth crossing. At 09.26, one minute later than scheduled, *Star Mist* took off bound for Dakar, by way of a refuelling stop in Lisbon. It arrived in West Africa around eighteen hours later at 00.48. Normally after a break of an hour or two the service would have resumed but for some reason – probably a technical problem with the aircraft; Yorks were always going out of service – passengers and crew were now delayed for a day. When their journey resumed it was in a different York, *Star Venture*, which took off at the ungodly hour of 02.43. There was little choice. If they had delayed until sunrise they would have arrived in Rio de Janeiro in the middle of the night. It was always better to start in darkness than finish in darkness. This way they arrived in time for supper and a night's sleep at Rio's Hotel Serrador overlooking the broad sweep of Botafogo Bay, where waiters in white gloves poured cold beer into frosted glasses. The next day promised more civilized departure times. *Star Venture* left Rio at 11.53. It stopped off in Montevideo to refuel and finally arrived at Morón airport in Buenos Aires at 20.25 on 1 August 1947.

Waiting for the crew at Morón was the Lancastrian *Star Dust*, registration G–AGWH, one of BSAA's very first aircraft. Bennett took possession of it in January 1946, the same month as the first ever BSAA flight. It commenced commercial flying in March 1946 and up to 2 August 1947 had flown a little over 1,655 hours for the company. Three of *Star Dust*'s engines, all Rolls-Royce Merlins of various but similar vintages, had been overhauled within the last 600 hours of service. The fourth was a little newer and had seen only 535 hours of service altogether. *Star Dust* was not, by anybody's standards, an old aircraft.

It was also one of the few BSAA planes to boast a name ripe with cultural resonances. The 'Star' prefix adopted by the airline had produced a number of hefty and heroic monikers which suited the pioneering, technological spirit of the age. There was nothing at all fey or embarrassing about a plane called *Star Lion* or *Star Eagle* or *Star Glory*, but as time went on and the fleet grew, the search for appropriate names had become slightly desperate. There were, among the BSAA roster, *Star Olivia* and *Star Visitant*, *Star Dew* and even *Star Pixie*.

Star Dust, by contrast, immediately referred to something: the soft lilting melody of the same name by the great Hoagy Carmichael, with lyrics by Mitchell Parish. The song was made famous by Benny Goodman and Glenn Miller and in the two decades since the late 1920s when it was written had become a copper-bottomed standard. It was, to all intents and purposes, the very first pop song. The wealthy BSAA passengers, mostly people just like Pagh and Gooderham, would have been more than familiar with its unashamedly romantic tones played endlessly in the exclusive piano and cocktail bars of the world. The words too, with their references to dusk and twilight, to love and separation, to the great dome of the star-pricked night sky, had their own particular appeal. Over the months since *Star Dust* went into service, few passengers striding across the airfield towards the waiting aircraft would have failed to notice its name, printed high on the nose beneath the cockpit window.

At Morón the remaining post for Santiago was loaded into the hold, alongside a large consignment of French feature films, subtitled in Spanish and destined for the movie-hungry Chilean market. After the luggage it was the largest single item of cargo, weighing in at a little over 53 pounds. Other than that the manifest showed only a package of some 6 pounds containing objects made from Bakelite being dispatched to the Chilean capital by a P. Meyer. There was nothing else, and certainly no gold. In total the aircraft weighed 51,356 pounds, a long way below its maximum take-off weight of 65,000 pounds.

Before he departed Reginald Cook was given the weather chart. It was not the most useful of documents: rather than showing what was to come it showed what had been. Specifically it showed the situation at 20.00 the day before departure. At that point, while the air as far as Mendoza was clear enough, the situation in the Andes was appalling. Snow storms were raging and turbulence was moderate to intense. From the air, the report said, you could neither see the ground nor fly on instruments. That, of course, was what *had* been happening. Cook would only find out what was going on today when he got there. He was informed once again that if the weather was bad over the mountains he should divert to the north or the south of the direct route.

At 13.46 on 2 August 1947 *Star Dust* departed Buenos Aires for Santiago. Whatever Jack Leche had said about previous flights making dangerous economies on aviation fuel, this one at least was good and full. It was carrying 1,380 gallons of fuel, enough for a flight time of 6 hours and 30 minutes; the flight time to Santiago was just 3 hours and 45 minutes. According to the flight plan Cook filed, the trip across to Mendoza, a distance of 536 miles, would take 3 hours and 12 minutes. That would leave just a short hop of 106 miles across the peaks to Santiago, which would take the remaining 33 minutes. At 15.07 Denis Harmer radioed the ground that the *Star Dust* was at 10,000 feet, flying at a speed of 196 knots. The estimated time of arrival in Santiago was 17.30, bang on schedule. A little under an hour later he sent almost exactly the same message using Morse code, in which form all messages would now come. They were on track and, as far as they were concerned, making headway. By 17.00 they would, quite reasonably, have believed themselves to be over Mendoza although they could not have checked visually. The ground was completely obscured by cloud. According to the message Harmer now delivered, *Star Dust* was at 20,000 feet and climbing to 24,000 feet to cross the mountains. The estimated time of arrival had been put back to 17.43. Back in the cabin the passengers should already have been sucking down oxygen from the tubes delivered from overhead to compensate for the thin atmosphere. If they were not already doing so Iris Evans should have been working her way along, her portable 20-minute oxygen tank in hand, making sure everybody knew how to use the tube.

At 17.33 there was another message from Harmer to the radio operators on the ground at Los Cerrillos airport on the southern outskirts of Santiago. The arrival time was being put back a further two minutes to 17.45. Eight minutes later at 17.41 came a message repeating the arrival time. It ended with the letters S.T.E.N.D.E.C., battered out very fast in Morse code. The radio operator on the ground did not recognize the term: stendec was no form of short-hand he had ever seen, certainly not in this part of the world. He asked Harmer to repeat his message and back it came twice, loud, clear and fast.

S.T.E.N.D.E.C.

S.T.E.N.D.E.C.

And then . . .

And then, nothing. No sharp whirring of overexcited engines. No dull booming thud, nor any flames in the distance to illuminate the bleak Santiago dusk. Just an absence: a silence on the radio and a brooding empty sky. An absence that became more ominous and more deathly the longer it continued until the men in the radio tower could no longer avoid the crushing truth. They had lost her.

Star Dust was down.

CHAPTER FIFTEEN

LOLA ARRIVED AT LOS CERRILLOS AIRPORT IN SANTIAGO TO meet her husband around 17.30. Just after the plane's scheduled arrival time she was told by airport officials that it was delayed. It would be here in ten minutes, they said. Nothing to worry about. Only a short hold-up. The ten minutes passed. They became fifteen. And then twenty. The mood at Los Cerrillos changed, from expectant and businesslike to edgy and uncertain, as staff rushed with deliberate intensity about the building. Lola tried to find out what was happening, tried desperately hard. But all they would tell her was that they had lost contact with the plane. They were waiting to hear. They would come back to her the moment they knew something. Please be patient.

For officials of both the airport and the airline the conclusion should have been obvious, but they were haunted by the insidious temptations of hope. The last message from the *Star Dust* came just four minutes before it was due to arrive. By that time it should have been well clear of the mountains and out over the populated hills that surround the city. If it had come down there, by now somebody would have been on the telephone to announce a crash: fires lighting the night air, the sickly sweet smell of aviation fuel, the bang and crack of oxygen tanks bursting in the heat. But there was just that silence. And didn't the plane have almost three hours' more flying time in its tanks? Perhaps it had suffered some sort of radio failure. Maybe they were still up there in the clouds, now heading out over the sea, trying to get their bearings. It was not unknown for pilots lost over obscured coastal airfields to fly out to sea on the compass and then drop down through the cloud base. That way they could have a straight run back to the shore at low altitude, certain there was only flat water beneath them. They had to wait. They had to give the *Star Dust* a chance before jumping to conclusions.

At midnight Lola was told to go home and wait for a call, but she couldn't simply do nothing. Instead she went first to BSAA's offices in the centre of Santiago. She stood there on a deserted, night-empty city street, banging on the locked door, begging for information the anxious employees did not have to give. She returned home and stayed awake until daylight. At 07.00 the call came. *Star Dust* was officially missing.

By then Los Cerrillos airport had been on a state of emergency for many hours. Throughout the night radio operators tried desperately to raise the aircraft in the hope that she had been forced to put down somewhere fifty miles away either to the north or to the south, but there was not a sound. They left the Eureka beacon pulsing its staccato message to the airwaves in the vain, frankly ludicrous hope that she was still up there, in the clouds, looking for them. Soon attention turned to the mountains where, for days now, blizzards had been raging. One report said the aircraft had put down in Mendoza for a few hours before taking off again and heading for the northern path, but it later turned out not to be true. Another report claimed she had been seen flying over the great statue of Christ which stands high in the mountains, its arms outstretched, marking the Argentine–Chilean border.

At daybreak on 3 August the Chilean army ordered troops from the mountain station at Portillo, 9,000 feet up on the slopes, to brave the storms and begin a search of the snowfields on skis. Over at the Colina military base three aircraft of the Chilean air force were dispatched to fly through the high passes. They were joined by aircraft from the Argentinian air force over on the other side. Private flying clubs and mountaineering groups on both sides of the border organized their own search parties and soon an area of over 250 square miles was being scoured for wreckage or, better still, survivors.

The news broke in Britain on 4 August. 'British plane missing' reported a headline in the *Manchester Guardian*. Beneath that, in smaller print, was the plaintive subheading 'Last Heard in Andes'. In *The Times* it was 'Search for *Star Dust*'. The newspapers held out the hope that the aircraft had made a forced landing. The plucky South American troops, even now forcing their way through driving snow and high winds, might eventually be able to rescue the eight Britons and three other foreign nationals from the slopes of the Andes. There was always a chance. On 6 August *The Times* published another story. According to His Majesty's Postmaster General, the short article said, all the letters from Britain to Chile sent at the end of July had been on board the BSAA aircraft. The *Star Dust* was described at the end of the report as simply 'overdue'.

In Limpsfield, Surrey, Jack Gooderham's brother-in-law Fred bashed out a telegram to Jack's brother Paddy in Johannesburg. 'Jack plane reported missing,' it said. 'No definite news will advise any further developments.' Elsewhere in Surrey Paul Simpson's niece, Christine, was in the bath when there was a knock at the front door. It was answered by one of her parents and she heard the visitor's voice echoing up the stairwell towards her. 'Have you heard?' it said. 'Paul's plane has gone missing. It was on the radio.' In Bedford Peter Young's nieces were outside on a blisteringly hot summer's day, stamping on tar bubbles, when the radio news bulletin reached them. The family gathered round to listen. Young was listed by name as among the missing and his sister promptly fainted. His mother refused to believe he was dead. The man on the wireless had talked about a 'forced landing', she said. Peter was alive, somewhere, up there in the mountains. She was sure of it. They would find him. The house fell silent that summer, but wafting over from other radio sets in other front parlours came the popular songs of the day. Among them they could hear Carmen Miranda singing 'South American Way', with an almost mocking irony.

Harald Pagh's brother Julius received the news a few days later when he and his family arrived in Fjallbacka, Sweden, for their summer holiday. It came in a telegram from a friend of Pagh's called Herbert Zucker. 'Desolated being unable rendering any aid your unfortunate brother Harald,' it read, in the curiously fractured language used for economy's sake in telegrams. 'Had first news august fourth quote pagh disappeared aircrash unquote . . . press-reports claim expeditions airplanes trying find debris without result as mountains all snowcovered be assured my deepest sympathies also your mother and your sister.' Zucker had no doubt. Pagh was gone.

By the time Julius Pagh received his telegram Don Bennett was already in Buenos Aires remonstrating with the Argentinian authorities who, like the Chileans, had abandoned the search after almost a week. They knew all about the mountains. They knew what the chances of survival were, particularly in August. There was, they said, no point in continuing. Bennett wasn't having it. He remembered the rescue of a pilot from the snowfields of Newfoundland during the Atlantic Ferry days. Chaps could survive for a long time, if they had the will. The moment to give up on them had not yet come. He collected the BSAA Lancastrian stationed at Montevideo to freight spare parts about for the company in the region and told two pilots, Archie Jackson and Frank Taylor, that they would help him crew the aircraft for the search. A Stargirl, Paddy Powers, and a few local employees were ordered to come along too so that they could scan the mountainsides from the Lancastrian's windows. Before they departed he loaded the plane with supplies packed in bright red boxes plus a pair of skis and a parachute. When the *Star Dust* was found, he told his quietly bemused staff, he would naturally jump out of the aircraft and go to their aid.

They landed first at Mendoza where the airport officials told Bennett the mountain passes were closed by low cloud, but the air vice-marshal would not be put off by a little low cloud. He would go and look anyway, he told them. It was the least his passengers and crew deserved. Soon they were flying beneath the bruising cloud base, with the sheer walls of the mountains closing in on either side of them. Suddenly Bennett pulled what was known to his pilots as a sharp 'split arse' turn so that for a moment they were pointed right at the mountain face and flying towards it at well over a hundred miles per hour.

Taylor turned to Jackson. 'If you haven't written your will,' he said, 'I think now would be a good time.'

Despite the hours spent in the air nothing was found. Bennett refused to be put off. They would continue searching, he said, and they would leave each day at first light. One morning, as they gathered at the Mendoza airfield, a number of the crew suggested they take a few minutes to get a little breakfast before setting off.

Bennett was furious. 'All you people think about is your stomachs,' he shouted. 'Have you no concern for those poor people in the mountains?'

Now it was Paddy Powers's turn to lose her temper. 'They have all been dead for days,' she barked. 'We are the ones who are threatened with starvation.'

Over on the other side of the Andes in Santiago a former BSAA employee called James Storey was also searching for the *Star Dust*. Storey had been a flight lieutenant during the war and a post-war desk job with the company had only given him an itch to get back in the air. Early in 1947 he bought a Spitfire of his very own from the RAF for £500. He fitted it with extra tanks and flew it across the south Atlantic to Argentina where, he announced, he would make a killing from aerial survey work. But nobody wanted him to survey anything. By the time of the *Star Dust*'s disappearance he was the proud owner of a Spitfire which was doing nothing but eat a deep hole in his pocket. Now the BSAA manager in Buenos Aires, Wing Commander Trevor Waymouth, remembered Storey and his Spitfire. He asked him if he would be prepared to help in the search for the lost aircraft. Storey agreed and, in return for expenses and around £5 a day, based himself at the Carrera Hotel in Santiago. Each morning he took his Spitfire out into the tight mountain passes and flew low over the snowfields and glaciers. It was risky flying performed without the small peace of mind offered by a parachute; his had been stolen at Dakar and he had not been able to replace it. All he had beneath his seats were two empty parachute bags. The risks he took did not pay off. Like Bennett's Lancastrian flying out of Mendoza, he found nothing. Each night he returned to the Carrera and the solace of the hotel bar where the local BSAA staff met to drink and share their gloomy theories.

At the Carrera the view of what had happened to the *Star Dust* was clear and simple: Reginald Cook was on his first command. He had been determined to get through. He didn't want to let Bennett down by taking a diversion that would have cost BSAA dear. So Cook had gone for it, ploughing into filthy weather over the peaks. An old hand would not have tried to cross the Andes, they said. An old hand would have put in to Mendoza and stayed there. An old hand would still be alive. It was a question of experience. The *Star Dust* was gone.

The family of Casis Said Atalah was not so easily convinced. At least $10,000 was offered as a reward to anybody who could provide any information at all about what had happened. On whispers and rumours Lola's family and friends mounted search expeditions up into the mountains that went on for weeks. Nothing was found. Far away in Bethlehem his mother lay dying. She was told that her son's plane was missing and she declared that her life could not come to an end until she knew exactly what had happened to him. For weeks she lingered on the edge of death. Eventually, to ease her pain, her family went to her bedside and announced that her beloved Casis had been found alive and well. Two days later she died.

On 15 August Harald Pagh's company, Wollimex of Zürich, issued a statement to his many friends and business associates around the world. 'It is our sad duty to let you know that our managing director, Mr Harald Pagh, has been missing since 2 August 1947,' the statement, written in French, began. It listed the route his journey had followed, wrongly asserting that the *Star Dust* had landed at Mendoza before heading for Santiago. 'We are horrified by the thought that our Mr Pagh may not be coming back,' it concluded, 'but the reports we have received lead us to fear the worst. It is extremely painful for us to give you this news and we will be sure to keep you informed as we get more precise details.'

That same day at BSAA's offices in Buenos Aires Trevor Waymouth received startling news: a chauffeur, a businessman and a landowner up in Calingasta, 180 miles to the north of Mendoza, were all reporting having seen a large silver aircraft flying high towards the mountains on the day of the disappearance. Waymouth and the British embassy's air attaché, Squadron Leader Alan Craig, went up there the very next day in the embassy plane and searched the valleys. They discovered nothing, save that the area was appallingly mapped. Valleys which were shown as being fifteen miles wide were often little more than two. Mapmaking mistakes like that could have explained a lot, Craig later reported back to the embassy.

But what Craig could not explain was what the *Star Dust* would have been doing so far to the north of its normal route. He put his doubts to Waymouth who eventually decided to confide in the diplomat. As Craig later explained in a memo to his superiors which was stamped 'Top Secret', one of the highest security classifications, BSAA crews were not always completely honest about which route they were intending to use. 'Because of difficulties with the Argentine authorities BSAA crews used a Northerly Route on days of bad weather, although putting in a flight plan for a direct route,' Craig said, quoting Waymouth. 'They did this rather than face the alternative of cancelling the flight. However, to maintain secrecy over this plan the

Captain leaving Buenos Aires . . . was not even expected to inform the local BSAA authorities of his actual intentions. If he took the northerly route he would still send his position signals as though he was on the direct route.' If the Argentine authorities were ever to find out about this flagrant disregard for regulations, Craig concluded, British aviation in South America would be in serious trouble. 'For this reason [this] report has been graded TOP SECRET.'

It was a startling revelation and one that officials in the Civil Aviation Ministry back in London refused to believe. There were established alternatives to the direct route readily available. The Argentinians had approved them. Why use another route, which would, as one official put it, be a 'thoroughly dangerous procedure'? When Craig went back to Waymouth to clarify the issue the BSAA station manager tried to backtrack a little. BSAA pilots wouldn't exactly have lied when they gave their position, he said. They would say something like 'longitude Mendoza', and they would indeed have been on exactly the same longitude as Mendoza – just 180 miles to the north of the city.

'It seems to me,' Craig concluded in November 1947, 'that Waymouth, presumably out of loyalty to his company, was attempting to prepare British officials for finding *Star Dust* well off its planned route in view of the strong rumours that the aircraft had been seen [around Calingasta].' It was a wasted effort on Waymouth's part. The wreck was not found in the area.

In the early autumn of that year, however, reports began to appear in the British press announcing that the aircraft had indeed finally been located. *The Times* went so far as to declare that an expedition of Chilean policemen was setting off from Parral, south of Santiago, to reach the crash site. It was, the paper said with some authority, at an altitude of 9,700 feet in the Andes. The reports were completely untrue and on 9 October 1947 BSAA wrote to Jack Gooderham's parents telling them so.

'You may have seen in the press within the last day or so reports that the missing aircraft *Star Dust* had been located,' wrote the company secretary, a Mr Porter. 'I much regret to inform you that these reports are without foundation. In view of the time that has now elapsed since the aircraft was first reported missing there can, I regret to say, be no hope now of finding any survivors. I am endeavouring to obtain certificates of presumption of death to enable the estates of all concerned to be dealt with.' He promised to get in touch immediately if there was any other news.

In the weeks immediately following the loss of the *Star Dust* BSAA suffered two more crashes, although they were small ones, at least by the company's standards. Only one crew member and one passenger sustained injuries and they were slight. That may have been pure luck: both aircraft were seriously damaged. The lack of corpses did little to reassure the Civil Aviation Ministry. It decided the time had come to carry out in-depth research on AVM Don Bennett's airline, the flying outfit which he said had a better safety record than Bomber Command. Up in Whitehall's government offices statisticians went to work, studying the period from 1 January 1946 to the end of August 1947. Their findings were startling. For every 100 million passenger miles that BSAA's rival airline BOAC had flown,

2.3 passengers had died in crashes. All the North American carriers put together had lost 3.78 passengers over the same distance. BEA, the British airline servicing domestic and European routes, had a clean slate. No passengers had died on any of their aircraft at all.

For BSAA the number of passengers lost per 100 million miles was 61.6.

Now the statisticians looked at passengers killed for passengers carried. BEA had carried 342,502 passengers without any loss. With BOAC one passenger had died for every 18,900 flown.

BSAA was killing one passenger for every 385 that they flew. It is the equivalent today of one passenger on board every full Boeing 747. It seemed that the last line of that dark, bitter joke about the comparative safety record of all the British airlines was true. BSAA really did spend more time than the other companies informing the next of kin.

CHAPTER SIXTEEN

Tupungato, High Andes

January 2000

ALEJO MOISO STUDIED THE MAP. AFTER THE FRUITLESS searching of the first expedition almost a year before there was just one segment of Tupungato left to explore. It broke down neatly into three separate routes. Of those one was clearly more challenging than the others, a harder ascent up tougher rock and ice. It made sense, Alejo said, to do the hardest job first. That way they could be guaranteed to have the strength to get through it. Sergeant Cardozo agreed. Up here at altitude their bodies would tire quickly, however fit they were. Better to get the difficult tasks over and done with. At 08.00 on their first full day at base camp the two men gathered up their climbing equipment and said their farewells to José. On a climb as arduous as this he would only have held them back and he knew it. He would be remaining behind.

'I wasn't disappointed not to be going,' José said later,

when they had come down off the mountain. 'My son is an extension of me. He went in my place.' He knew that without him, the expedition would not have happened; his credit for any discovery was secure and, to José, credit was what mattered.

The two men marched away upwards, stopping occasionally to study the slopes above them through binoculars. For hour after hour they saw nothing worthy of their attention save the mountain they were climbing. It was 14.00 before they spotted anything at all and even then it was indistinct: just a glimmer from the surface of the huge glacier that tumbled down off the peak towards them. Whatever they were looking at, whatever had caught the sunlight, it wasn't ice and it wasn't rock. It was also a fair distance away, perhaps as much as 3,000 metres. It would take time to get up there and time was now in short supply. It had taken them six hours to get this far, puffing through the thin air, and it would take hours to get back down again. If they left it too late they would be making the descent in darkness, a hazardous venture on any mountain, a potentially lethal one on Tupungato. Spending the night on the mountain was not an option because they were travelling light. They had no tent and no sleeping bags with which to endure the fiercely cold temperatures. The only refuge was back down with José and the other soldiers at the 2,000-metre base camp. Alejo and Sergeant Cardozo talked it over, but both of them knew what the decision would be. They had come too far, expended too much energy and too much hope, to turn back now. They had to go on.

'Yes, we took a risk,' Alejo said afterwards. 'We knew that the return would be complicated.' But then what is mountaineering without risk? Nothing but a long, hard walk uphill.

It was Alejo who made the first find: a copper oxygen bottle, a little dented but intact for all that, just lying there on the frozen ground at 4,800 metres. He was euphoric. It had to belong to the Lancastrian. Only an unpressurized aircraft would carry an oxygen tank like this and the only unpressurized aircraft still missing in the Andes was the Lancastrian. Slowly they began working their way up the slope. Fragments were scattered everywhere, just as Reguera and Garmendia had said they were. Here were small shards of the fuselage and there, embedded in the mountain ice, were pieces of cloth. They pulled at the rags to get them free but all the cloth did was tear and then break down into threads that fluttered away on the mountain breeze. Sergeant Cardozo moved about the moraine picking up the different objects he found, for the most part scraps of the aircraft's metallic shell. He waved them at Alejo and asked him to identify the pieces. The soldier knew about mountains and what they could do to climbers who didn't respect them, but he knew nothing about wreckage like this. Alejo answered as best he could but he was distracted. What he wanted to find, needed to find even, was anything that could give them positive proof they really were looking at the wreckage of the *Star Dust*. However hard he looked he could see nothing like that anywhere.

It was almost 16.30 when they arrived at the site.

Together they decided that, whatever happened, they would leave again at 18.00. No arguments. They would still end up descending in darkness – that was now unavoidable – but at least they might make it back down to base camp before the coldest stretch of the night.

It was just as they were preparing to turn back that they started finding the pieces of bone. There was no doubt about it. These were human. They continued climbing the slope and then moved up on to a section of the glacier itself, following a trail of bone fragments scattered across the rock and ice. Lying on the surface of the glacier they found a human torso complete with one arm and hand. It was a creamy shade of calcified white but there was no mistaking what it was: a body that had lain here for a very long time indeed, both exposed to and protected by the elements. Before they could say anything further to each other Sergeant Cardozo dropped to his knees. There, beside the human remains, he began to pray. The younger man watched him for a moment. Alejo was not religious, but that didn't mean he had to be disrespectful. Slowly he dropped down on to his knees as well so that he could, as he put it later, 'accompany him in his prayer'.

It was a useful pause. All those years that he and his father searched for the *Star Dust* there had been one picture fixed in Alejo's mind: a classic plane wreck, complete with lumps of wing and propellers buried in the hard earth and perhaps a little cargo cracked open and scattered about. And, of course, those bars of butter-yellow gold spilling out of their box. Nowhere in those images had there been space for dead bodies. And yet, instead of gold, here was a torso with an arm and a hand. Quietly his friend continued to offer up his devotion. When he was done they both stood up and started looking about for other human remains. They soon found them. In all they counted three torsos lying around the glacier plus a single hand, severed at the wrist, the fingers curled upwards as though beckoning to someone. From the size of it, Sergeant Cardozo said, it looked like it had belonged to a woman. Alejo agreed. They left all the remains where they had first seen them and, with the light already beginning to fail, decided the time had finally come to get down the mountain.

Almost 3,000 metres below, José was surveying the slopes through the fast-falling darkness for any sign of the soldier and his son. It was late, far too late. José knew all too well that the mountain was fractured by crevices; if one of them fell in the other would struggle to get him out again. None of them had radios, and, in any case, with night coming it would be impossible to mount any kind of search. By morning it would be too late. For hour after hour José stood outside his tent, staring up at the fading silhouette of the mountain, willing them down.

It was 22.00 by the time Alejo and Sergeant Cardozo made it back to base camp. Night fell, bringing with it a full moon to light their way: a small comfort. Alejo, calmer now after the initial shock of their find, whispered the news to his relieved father. He did not want to be overheard by the two other soldiers who had accompanied them to base camp. He didn't want to announce the discovery to them until they were absolutely certain that it was the *Star Dust*.

'I think we've found it,' he said quietly. No, there wasn't

any gold, not that they had seen. But there was something else: body parts.

The next day the two men rested and took the time to describe in detail to José the various things they had seen: the pieces of fuselage and the oxygen tank, the shreds of cloth and the bone fragments. They estimated it was spread over a wide area up there, possibly as much as two square miles. They had to make at least one more trip up to the site, no doubt about it. José agreed. This time they should try to make a positive identification, José said, find something that would confirm it was the *Star Dust*.

The following day's climb was much quicker than it had been two days before. Their bodies were better acclimatized to the altitude now and they didn't need to stop so often. And they knew where they were going. It was not long after they had got there that Alejo came across the aircraft's identification plates. This was exactly what he needed. With the registration code printed on them Gustavo Marón could identify the plane for certain. He slipped them away into his pack. Nearby were a few documents but when he picked them up to see what they were the paper simply disintegrated in his hands. A few scraps remained intact but any writing they held was completely illegible. The two men separated out and started exploring the mountainside in detail. They came across no more body parts but there were other relics. There were twisted lumps of aluminium stamped with the British crown and a leather suitcase with the words 'Made in England' embossed near the lock.

Sergeant Cardozo picked up another piece of leather and

turned it over in his hands. Eventually he shouted across that he had found a boot. Alejo asked if there was anything printed on it. The soldier examined it closely again. On the sole he found three letters: RAF. 'Maybe it's the name of the manufacturer,' Alejo said. It was only later, when they had come down off Tupungato, that Alejo realized his mistake; that the letters stood for the Royal Air Force. 'Maybe the altitude was getting to me,' he said later.

A boot was a good find but what Alejo really wanted, what José had told him to look out for, was the engine that Reguera and Garmendia had first come across. That was nowhere to be seen. They clambered up on to the slope of the glacier and trudged upwards. Soon the *penitentes* were rising up around them, becoming larger and larger the further up they went until they were six metres tall. The sun was high overhead now and melting the ice so that lumps of the great pinnacles crashed down about them, shattering as they landed. Beneath their feet they could hear meltwater running off down the mountainside, and around them cracks and snaps echoed off the slopes and gullies as the ice shifted.

'This is a crazy thing,' Sergeant Cardozo said. 'We're actually standing inside the glacier. Let's get out of here.'

'No,' Alejo said. 'I want to stay. Let's just go a little further.'

Unwillingly, Sergeant Cardozo agreed. 'If one of us falls into the crevices up here nothing will get us out,' he said.

Alejo laughed. 'If you fall in you're staying in.'

They moved on, from one find to the next, from one piece of aircraft or cargo to another, until 700 metres from the first pieces of wreckage they finally found the engine, still perched on its pedestal of ice. It carried the words '-OLLS ROYCE' on the side, just as the two climbers from Tandil had described it. The reason they had thought it was a small engine and therefore a small aircraft was soon obvious. What they were looking at was only a third of the whole. The rest had clearly been cut away, probably in the original crash, and was nowhere to be seen. Sergeant Cardozo took a photograph of his companion squatting down next to the section of engine, a look of quiet satisfaction on his face. His father had been right. José Moiso's reputation was assured and to Alejo nothing mattered more.

Nearby was something Alejo found extraordinarily familiar: sticking out of the ground was one of the aircraft's four huge propellers, the long, spindle blades intact. In the centre was the cone-shaped hub. As a child Alejo went often with his father to the *Museo Nacional de Aeronautica* on the edge of the Jorge Newbery airport in Buenos Aires, where decommissioned aircraft sit on the neatly cropped lawns that look out over the broad river Plate. Among the exhibits is a complete Avro Lincoln, its long boxy fuselage and double tailfin proof that it was just another version of the original Lancaster bomber design that had made the company's name. Alejo had stared up at the aircraft often enough. He had memorized its contours and its shapes and its details so that standing here now before this massive propeller it was unmistakable. It was the same as the ones he had seen as a child. It had to have been made by the British company A.V. Roe Ltd. That meant only one thing. They really had found the wreck of the *Star Dust*.

CHAPTER SEVENTEEN

THEY ARRIVED BACK AT THE ELEVENTH MOUNTAIN REGIMENT'S base in the Andean foothills on 21 January 2000. It should have been a time for back-slapping and grand toasts. It should have been a time for celebration. José had long insisted that the wreck was up there, somewhere. He had cajoled and nagged and pushed to get the resources he needed to prove it. And now, after years of searching, the *Star Dust* had been found. He had done something remarkable. There was just one problem: a big celebration meant releasing the news of the find to the world and that was something the Moisos didn't want to do, not yet. As far as they were concerned, they said to Sergeant Cardozo, the only person who had to know right now was Gustavo Marón. Let the historian listen to the information they had gathered. Let him consider the facts and pore over the details. That was the way to proceed. The search had already taken them so long. Why rush things now?

Later there were those associated with the search for the *Star Dust* who questioned the motives of the Moisos and, in particular, of José himself. Why did he want to keep the news of the find so restricted, they asked. Was José merely after the legendary gold? Was that what the desire for secrecy was all about?

It would be a neat and tidy explanation. There is certainly no question that he believed the Lancastrian to be carrying bullion. He had studied the history, he would tell his friends. At the time of the crash Britain was buying large amounts of beef from Argentina but the Argentine government was not willing to accept payment in sterling because of its perceived weakness. As a result, José explained, they demanded instead that they be paid in gold. His reading of history was almost right. The Argentine government did indeed suspend sterling convertibility in August 1947 – but not until the twentieth of that month, a full two weeks after the *Star Dust* crashed. In any case if the gold was destined for banks in Buenos Aires what was it doing on board a plane bound for Santiago? It was going to banks elsewhere in Latin America, was all José would say.

Despite all of that José has never stated publicly that he had ambitions to get his hands on the gold; there is no reason, therefore, to attribute his apparent secrecy to a desire for financial gain. (Nevertheless he could be forgiven for thinking that such an intriguing aviation find would bring him enough reward – either mountaineering work or consultancy – to release him from his day job.) He did have another concern, however, and it was one which was to prove entirely justified. He feared that if he did not control how the news of the discovery was released then the credit for the find that he believed he and his son fully deserved would go to others.

The problem for the Moisos was the third member of the team. Sergeant Cardozo might be a friend and a fellow *andinista* but he was still a soldier. He had duties and, no matter what the Moisos said, he was obliged to abide by them. The first thing he did on arriving back at the base was to inform his commanding officer that, high up on Tupungato, he and his colleagues had found both wreckage and human remains. The news was passed up the chain of command to Lieutenant Colonel Bustos, commander of the Eleventh Mountain Regiment. He told the Moisos that the information would have to be reported to the judicial authorities because of the bodies, which meant some form of public announcement would also have to be made.

'The civilians wanted to keep the information quiet,' Lieutenant Colonel Bustos said a few months later, looking back on the whole affair. 'I said I couldn't. I explained I had my responsibilities.'

José says he was only concerned about the way the media would deal with the story. 'We didn't want it to become some big show. We didn't want people to come and treat the situation as if it were a butcher's shop window. We wanted to show a little respect for the families of the victims up there.' In any case, José says, at that point they didn't yet have the official confirmation that it was the *Star Dust*.

'I only said that it *could be* the *Star Dust*,' Lieutenant Colonel Bustos responds. 'We made that very clear to everybody.'

The find was officially reported to the federal judge in Mendoza, Alfredo Rodríguez, on 27 January 2000. Judge Rodríguez would decide what happened next. By then he needed only to open his local newspaper, *Los Andes*, to read the details. The first news stories appeared in the Mendoza press on 24 January. The day after that the news was all over the world. In many of the reports the discovery was attributed to a 'civilian–military' team.

'At the beginning of the search they didn't trust us,' José says, furiously. 'I had to beg them for support. And then suddenly, when we find the wreck, it became the army's discovery. They didn't give us the full credit.' It was slipping away from them.

The *Guardian* which, as the *Manchester Guardian*, had reported the *Star Dust*'s disappearance fifty-three years before, now announced its reappearance. 'Mystery of missing plane solved, 50 years on,' the headline said. The only member of the 'civilian–military search party' to be quoted was Cardozo. Through no fault of his own he was wrongly credited with initiating the search after the tip-off from Reguera and Garmendia. He was also described as sifting painstakingly through the archives and official records to identify which aircraft it might be lying up on Tupungato. 'The metal has turned all white and you could walk right by it without even noticing,' he was quoted as saying. 'Then we found clothes, cans and some human remains. The impact must have been terribly strong because the remains were mutilated and spread over a large area. Everything was perfectly frozen, including a woman's hand.'

Much of the reporting was confused and inaccurate. The BBC issued an account which gave the impression that both the aircraft and the victims' bodies were more or less intact. 'Inside the plane they found the bodies of three passengers perfectly preserved by the year-round freezing temperatures,' said a report on the broadcaster's website, dated 25 January. There was also a large amount of pure speculation. The day after the BBC report was released the international news agency Reuters, repeating information in local Argentinian newspapers, announced from Buenos Aires that 'an envoy of Britain's King George VI thought to be carrying secret documents was aboard'. By then the British government had made no comment on the contents of the diplomatic bag that Paul Simpson had been carrying. Elsewhere in the Argentinian press there were reports that the *Star Dust* had been carrying seventy bars of British gold when it crashed.

In Battersea, south London, a 75-year-old woman picked up her regular copy of the *Daily Telegraph* from the front door mat and read the first, short announcement of the find. She called the newspaper and asked to be put through to the news desk. She could supply a little information on one of the *Star Dust*'s crew, she said. She gave her name: Nina Brauer-Walton. A reporter and a photographer were dispatched and the article appeared in the *Telegraph* the next day under the headline 'Andes plane solves mystery of lost love'. As far as the newspaper was concerned Mrs

Brauer-Walton and Donald Checklin had been in the throes of a torrid love affair at the time of the crash. 'Mrs Brauer-Walton ... spoke yesterday of her distress when she discovered her boyfriend of only a few weeks had died in the crash,' the paper gushed. 'Mrs Brauer-Walton, who lived near Regents Park at the time, said she met Mr Checklin when she was 23. She said: "We went out for dinner and for drinks a few times. He was extremely good-looking and incredibly charming and gentle."' Entranced by this tale of burgeoning love sacrificed to the cruel fates, the world's media now descended on Mrs Brauer-Walton's small flat. For days her telephone did not stop ringing and the television camera crews kept coming. 'It was silly really,' she said later, when the interest had died away. 'He wasn't my boyfriend. He might have become my boyfriend later but he really wasn't at the time.'

At the grand, imposing building in London's Whitehall that is home to the British government's Foreign and Commonwealth Office, calls were now coming in from relations of both passengers and crew. All had thought that nothing more would ever be heard of people who had mostly become little more than curious footnotes in their family's history. There were calls from Christopher Cook, nephew of Hilton Cook, and from Mary Lowerson, niece of Peter Young. There was a phone call from Christine Reese, niece of Paul Simpson, and a letter from John Parker, brother-in-law of Reginald Cook. Some of the relations were scattered about the world. Harald Pagh's niece, the 'little Stella' of his last postcard from Buenos Aires, now lives in Pennsylvania, USA. Jack Gooderham's nephew, Paddy Gooderham, has made his home in western Canada. They all wanted to be kept in touch with developments as and when they happened.

The majority of these people found the news that the *Star Dust* had at last been found touching or poignant but little more. It brought back childhood memories, but only of the grief of adults; strong emotions that they were then too young to either understand or appreciate. Some saw it as little more than an intrigue, a mystery that had been solved. For Lola, widow of Casis Said Atalah, now in her eighties and still living in Santiago, it was so much more. It didn't matter that half a century had elapsed since her husband's disappearance. It didn't matter that her life had continued; that she had raised her four surviving children to successful adulthood. As the stories filled the Chilean newspapers, the reporters focusing on bizarre detail which for them seemed to intensify the curious romance of the tale, she began again to grieve. 'Part of me was happy when the wreck was discovered,' she said a few months after the find, 'because I finally knew where he was. But at the same time it has brought all the pain back.' She received nothing from BSAA after the crash, she said bitterly, no compensation, no support, not even a letter of condolence. Even now that the wreck had been found, she added, British Airways, the company which is in part descended from BSAA, had not seen fit to write to her to express their regret. All she had was silence. And she began to weep again. She had been doing a lot of weeping since she first heard the wreck had been found. That was what the discovery had done to her, she said.

She did see one benefit: at least she might now be able to get back her husband's remains. At least she might now be able to place him in a grave. A similar thought had occurred to a number of other relatives. For that to be at all practical, of course, the remains would first have to be identified. That meant DNA tests on what was left of the victims' bodies cross-matched to blood samples taken from the next of kin. Before they could be tested those remains would have to be brought down off the mountain. A few days after the discovery of the wreck was announced the British embassy in Buenos Aires sent a formal request to Judge Rodríguez asking for his assistance in recovering and then identifying the bodies. He accepted the request and passed it on to Colonel Mario Chretien, the overall commander of the Eighth Mountain Brigade, of which the Eleventh Mountain Regiment is a part.

Like many of those who rise to senior positions within the military, Colonel Chretien is a soldier who recognizes the wider social and political implications of the job he is called upon to perform. At the time of the discovery it was less than twenty years since the British and Argentinian armies had fought each other over the rocky, windswept Falklands/Malvinas islands. At the end of that bloody and painful war the Argentinian army had been forced to surrender to the British. Now Colonel Chretien was faced with what was, by anybody's standards, an opportunity. His army could prove its marvellous competence and professionalism by tackling the imposing Tupungato. They would be the ones to bring back the bodies of Britain's lost former Second World War bomber pilots.

It is significant that the Argentinian army did not wait for Judge Rodríguez to inform the British embassy of the find – as diplomatic etiquette would usually demand – but did so themselves, by two-page fax. As the Moisos had long ago recognized, there was a certain credibility to be gained from this find. Colonel Chretien wanted to make sure his organization received as much of it as possible.

Already Judge Rodríguez was being inundated with requests from the world's media for their journalists to be able to take part in any army expedition up Tupungato to recover the human remains. The British embassy in Buenos Aires had received no fewer than three separate requests from different parts of the BBC, each wanting to send their own television crews and reporters. Day by day the discovery of the *Star Dust* was turning into the perfect news story: there was romance and adventure, drama and mystery. What's more all the victims had been dead for over half a century. There was nothing there to upset the readers or the viewers too much. They could simply luxuriate in the narrative without becoming dispirited. News executives, who knew nothing of the grief Lola was suffering, saw the *Star Dust* story as the ideal antidote to the usual diet of human misery with which they generally filled their bulletins. As far as they were concerned it was news *lite*.

Judge Rodríguez decided the media requests would be passed on to Colonel Chretien. The colonel, although politically savvy, was not used to dealing with the media. It wasn't his job. Still, he could see the possibilities. Not only would his men be able to prove themselves against the very fiercest of elements, they could do so before ranks of admiring newsmen. 'It was marketing business for us,' he said afterwards. 'I had to ask for special authorization [from my superiors] to be allowed to do something like this. They agreed it was a special case.'

José Moiso watched developments with growing dismay. It was just as he had feared. What should have been a find of great historical significance was turning into a media circus. Finally, in early February, he decided he could stand by no longer. He filed an application with Judge Rodríguez demanding that the only team allowed up the mountain be a technical one who would know how to deal with both the bodies and the historical artefacts, and that the media be barred from Tupungato. The application was rejected. 'When we saw that the judge did not respect our position we knew the case was lost,' José says. 'When we find things on the mountains we are always very respectful. We do not remove them. Personally I wanted the bodies to stay where they were.'

And then he says: 'I do sometimes regret finding the site because of what happened next.' Neither José nor Alejo Moiso would take part in the army's expeditions. Instead, resentful and nursing understandable grievances, they would have to watch from Mendoza and follow developments in the media, just like everybody else. Their part in the long story of the *Star Dust* was over.

CHAPTER EIGHTEEN

ONLY A FEW DOZEN METRES FROM THE SPOT OCCUPIED BY THE Avro Lincoln that Alejo Moiso once so admired, at the *Museo Nacional de Aeronautica* in Buenos Aires, sits a sleek Douglas Skyhawk A–4B. At first glance it seems an odd exhibit to have at this museum. Most of the other aircraft on display are vintage machines just like the Lincoln, clunky propeller-driven planes with square fuselages and snub noses. And then there's the mighty Skyhawk, all fine lines and points and aerodynamic mouldings. It has a top speed of more than 1,000 miles per hour and can fly to a height of over nine miles. The reason for its presence here can be found on the fighter's nose, just below the cockpit canopy: three rather amateurish stencils of warships, in thick yellow paint. Beneath each one, in the same shade of custard yellow, is printed a name and a date. The first reads 'HMS Ardent, 21–05–82', the second 'HMS Argonaut

21–05–82' and lastly 'HMS Antelope 23–05–82'. Each one is a British warship destroyed during the Falklands/Malvinas War of 1982. Each one was sunk by this specific fighter. The Skyhawk is as close as a machine will ever get to being a war hero.

The museum is run by the Argentinian air force. That it should be content to display the Skyhawk like this, complete with a plaque noisily celebrating its achievements, is clear proof of the pride the air force takes in its performance during the Falklands/Malvinas War. It has good reason to do so. Many military experts accept that while the Argentinian army and navy were no match for the British task force, the well-trained pilots of the Argentinian air force inflicted serious damage, sinking ship after British ship. But the most important thing about the Falklands/Malvinas War, as far as the Argentinian air force is concerned, is this: that while the Argentinian army surrendered, they never did. The air force was, and remains, undefeated. Two decades on, that simple fact stands at the heart of a pronounced rivalry between these two wings of the Argentinian military. Now, thanks to a misunderstanding by Judge Rodríguez, the discovery of the *Star Dust* would bring that rivalry into grim relief.

Nearly 300 miles to the north-east of Mendoza is the city of Córdoba. Its ageing civil airport is just on the outskirts of the city and to one side of that airport is the region's largest air force base. Right out on the furthest edge of that air force base, housed in a set of scuffed and tatty blocks that could be mistaken for storage sheds, are the local offices of Argentina's Air Accident Investigation

Board (AAIB). The shabby impression is not helped by the large, twisted pieces of damaged aircraft that often sit in the overgrown pasture to the back of the block. At the time of the *Star Dust*'s discovery most of a private helicopter, bent and twisted and broken by its impact with the ground, was sitting out there like some wreck in a breaker's yard.

Officially the AAIB is a civilian organization although it works under the auspices of the air force, which provides most of its investigators on secondment. Carlos Sorini, who was born only a month after the disappearance of the *Star Dust* in 1947, is one of the few not to have served in the air force. It shows: his small compact body is clearly not one that has been through the hardships of boot camp and he has a wry, mischievous take on the machinations of the military with whom he must work. His mother was a pilot and in 1964, when he was just seventeen, he too took to the air, first learning to fly gliders. He moved on to light aircraft in 1968 when he was still just twenty-one. A year later he was helping to organize a local air show when one of the acrobatics pilots went into a corkscrew manoeuvre high over the airfield and failed to come out again. The plane crashed and exploded. The pilot was killed instantly.

'It was the first time I had seen an accident,' Sorini says now. 'And I wanted to know exactly why it had happened.' It was a long haul. There were qualifications to be gained and apprenticeships to be served. But eventually in 1982, a few months after the conclusion of the Falklands/Malvinas War, he was accepted into the AAIB. Since then he has investigated over 320 air accidents in Argentina and Bolivia: everything from small private planes and gliders to large commercial jets which have crashed with great loss of life.

Unlike the Moisos and Gustavo Marón, who had made it their life's work, Sorini had not previously been aware of the legend of the British Lancastrian lost to the Andes. The first he heard about it was from a journalist in Mendoza, who telephoned him in that third week of January 2000. 'He asked me if I knew anything about an accident in the mountains in 1947,' Sorini says. 'I had to tell him that I knew nothing about it at all.'

A little later that same day he received another call, this time from his superiors in Buenos Aires. They had seen the newspaper reports of the Moisos' find and they were in no doubt: it was a case for them. Ordinarily a 53-year-old wreck might not have required their attention. Their job – like that of air-accident investigators all over the world – is to assess air crashes so that, by learning from them, the same thing could be stopped from happening again. Aviation had moved on so far that there was hardly going to be much to learn from the shattered remains of an old Lancastrian, 4,800 metres up a mountain. But this case was different. There were body parts up there. What's more, it was clearly getting serious media attention. The board (and, by association, the air force) had to be involved, if only for form's sake. After all, it was their responsibility, not the army's. It should be treated like any other air crash, Sorini's bosses now told him, regardless of the years that had elapsed.

It was agreed that he would be joined on the investigation by Luis Estrella, a major in the air force who had been with the board since 1995. Major Estrella is a solidly built man in his forties who is now softening a little about the waist after a few years away from military life. He was an oddly appropriate choice for the job. His father was a navigator for the Argentinian air force serving on board Lancastrians and Lincolns. Estrella himself was almost born on board a Lancastrian when his mother went into labour during a flight from Córdoba to the city of Mercedes.

Sorini and Estrella now flew to Mendoza. Sorini asked for an appointment with Judge Rodríguez, who agreed to see him immediately. The investigator explained why he was in town. By law all air accidents are the responsibility of the AAIB, he said. They would take over the case from here. Judge Rodríguez faced a potentially embarrassing situation. According to the request for assistance that he had made to Colonel Chretien, total responsibility for the case had already been handed over to the army. A representative from the army was swiftly summoned to the judge's office in the central court building for an emergency meeting. Something had to be done. It was Sorini who suggested the compromise. The army would mount their expedition to recover the bodies from the mountain, but the AAIB would be responsible for the investigation. All sides agreed and the judge made one last stipulation: that the AAIB and the air force keep the army in touch with everything they were doing. The request was wildly optimistic. It presupposed a heart-warming degree of co-operation between the two wings of the military that had never previously existed.

Within hours the first fissure in the relationship showed itself, when Sorini went to talk over the details with the army. 'I asked for the coordinates of the crash site,' the investigator says. 'A little later I was studying a map when I realized the coordinates they had given me had to be completely wrong. They referred to a location over the border in Chile, well out of my jurisdiction and well out of theirs.'

Why would they do such a thing? 'I think they thought the air force would try to beat them to the crash site if they gave us the correct coordinates,' Sorini says. He had to go back to the army a second time before they would finally give him the correct coordinates.

Elsewhere in the army's headquarters on avenida San Martín, Colonel Chretien had been considering the requests from the media. Finally he decided that there was just one team which deserved special treatment. The BBC's science documentary series *Horizon* had asked to accompany the expedition for an extended film on the disappearance of the *Star Dust* which would also be shown by PBS in the United States. The producer, Jonathan Renouf, is an experienced amateur mountaineer. The cameraman, Sean Smith, was one of Britain's leading young mountaineers before moving into television where he has carved out a niche for himself by shooting footage from the top of some of the world's highest peaks. He would be flying in from the Himalaya for the job. On 10 February the British embassy contacted the *Horizon* team in London. Their request had been accepted, they were told, and all the other BBC requests refused. Provided they agreed to travel at their own risk and pay a fee of $5,000 on arrival in

Mendoza to cover costs incurred by the army, the three-man team could join the expedition. The BBC readily accepted the deal. They were told to be in town by 17 February. Another seventeen journalists were given the army's approval, many from Argentinian or Chilean newspapers and television. There were also journalists from the British press and from Reuters. Spanish television dispatched Miguel Moreno y Gil, one of the world's leading freelance cameramen. He had spent his career in the dirtiest and most dangerous war zones, watching people die horrible deaths. Now he would be climbing a mountain to find the bodies of those who were already long dead.

In the middle of February the journalists began arriving in Mendoza. Each one was charged $1,500. They were put through a medical and then, on their first evening, addressed by Lieutenant Colonel Bustos.

'This,' he told them, proudly, 'will show you the very finest the Argentinian army has to offer.' Next they were treated to an audio-visual presentation, full of sharp computer graphics, projected on to a screen from an army laptop. An image of a Lancastrian careered through a blue sky, like something from one of Terry Gilliam's animations for *Monty Python's Flying Circus*, before smacking into a graphic of the mountain, the impact marked by a cartoon explosion and sound effects. The route up the mountain then appeared before them, each slide slipping elegantly into the next as they were introduced to the mighty challenges they would face. As long as everybody did as they were told up on Tupungato, the officer said, everything would be fine.

'This is a good chance for us to improve relations between our two countries,' Lieutenant Colonel Bustos told the reporter from one British newspaper afterwards. And then, using the subtlest language a career soldier could be expected to muster, he said, 'Maybe if we give something back [to you], you will give something back to us, no?'

If the army thought any of the journalists were at all interested in the political ramifications of the expedition and its relevance to the Falklands/Malvinas War almost two decades before, they were sadly mistaken. Nor were they particularly interested in the challenge posed by Tupungato. What concerned them most was the other reporters they would be climbing with. Their newspapers and television stations had paid $1,500 to get them on to this expedition, a fair amount of cash even for the richest of media operations. As a result, the journalists were expected to deliver and they knew it. Their editors wanted good copy and good footage. And they wanted it first.

Soon most of the journalists realized they had a common enemy: the team from the BBC. It transpired there would be two expeditions. The first would be going up early to collect the remains. The second would follow on a day or so behind, and it was that one which most of the journalists would be allowed to join. 'It suddenly became clear to us that the BBC had somehow hitched themselves up with the advance party,' says Nicolás García, then a reporter for the Mendoza-based newspaper *Los Andes*. 'The BBC told us they wouldn't be screening anything for months so it didn't matter. But that wasn't good enough for many of the journalists. They were shouting at the army. They were saying things like, "What if they find the gold or the body of a German spy? If there's anything good to see up there the BBC is going to see it first." '

The army tried to reassure the rest of the press pack. The BBC team weren't news journalists, they said. They were making a documentary. It was a different thing entirely. The pack refused to be convinced. 'Then one morning while we were all kicking our heels in Mendoza,' García says, 'we suddenly realized the BBC team was nowhere to be seen. They had got away from us.' As far as the journalists left behind were concerned the army was playing games with them. Through sheer inexperience the military had managed to turn the media against them even before the expedition had begun.

It was only one of the army's problems. In a building on the edge of the small Mendoza airfield, home both to the local airport and a small detachment from the air force, Major Luis Estrella was hosting a secret briefing for a select few, and Colonel Chretien's Eighth Mountain Brigade wasn't invited. The second army expedition had not yet left town but Major Estrella didn't want to waste any time. He knew he had to move fast. The air force was going to attempt to get its helicopters to the crash site before the army arrived there on foot. They had asked Judge Rodríguez for permission and he had given it. Surely it wasn't the fault of the air force if nobody had thought to warn the army about it in advance?

It would not be an easy flight, Estrella now said. At that point they believed, mistakenly, that the wreckage lay 5,500 metres up Tupungato, which was at the very extreme of what a Lama helicopter could manage. The problem, the major said, was not so much getting up there, although that would be fraught with difficulty in itself. The real worry was whether the Lama would be able to take off again once it had landed. But, he said, he was sure it could be done.

At the end of his briefing he solemnly addressed his audience. In the room were a number of English-speaking journalists whom the air force was trying to lure away from the army's expedition, with the enticing prospect of arriving at the crash site first.

'My name is Estrella,' he now said in English, for their benefit. 'In English it means star. I hope I don't become star dust.'

CHAPTER NINETEEN

England

1947

BEFORE HE LEFT FOR SOUTH AMERICA JACK GOODERHAM wrote a letter which, he told his secretary, was to be given to his mother Elizabeth if anything happened to him. 'I think she will be giving it to her this week,' Jack's older sister Elsie wrote to her surviving brother Paddy, in the second week of October 1947. 'We have waited while there was hope but now I think she ought to have it. I hope to be there when she gets it as I quite expect she will be upset.'

She wrote to Paddy again, in early November. 'Isn't it strange him leaving it?' she said, of Jack's letter. 'It's the first time he has ever done such a thing. I did not see it as it's her letter. Anyhow it was telling her not to worry and to carry on until everything was settled and where the will was. Also that he had [had] a very happy life and thanking her for all she had been to him and the help she had given him to make it so.' Finally Elsie said: 'It looks as if Jack had an idea he would not come back.'

At least Elizabeth Gooderham was allowed the comfort of some last words from her son. Mary Checklin had nothing like that. There was just a hole in her life where her Donald had once been. Nurse Checklin's boys were everything to her. Nothing mattered more than them. And now one of them was gone. She began writing letters begging for help to find out exactly what had happened to the *Star Dust*. She needed to know what had become of him. She wrote to British embassies in Argentina and Chile, to the Foreign Office and the Civil Aviation Ministry and to BSAA itself. The responses, though sympathetic, offered no promise of help. She kept the replies on the mantelpiece of the heavy wooden fireplace at her home in West Bridgford, on the outskirts of Nottingham. When people came to call she would bring the letters down and insist they read them. She told George, Donald's brother, that it was also his duty to find out what had happened. He was a qualified geologist now and used to going to rough and inhospitable places. He should put his experience to good use, she said; Donald deserved it. George promised to do everything he could. Mary Checklin's friends and relatives tried to tell her that it was time to move on. Not that she should forget about Donald – she could never do that – but that she should try, at least, to start rebuilding her life as best she could. She didn't see it that way. She continued writing her letters right up until her death in September 1959.

Late in 1947 and early the next year both she and Reginald Cook's widow Cicely wrote similar letters to their respective members of Parliament. The pilots had been forced to fly for too many hours without rest, they told their MPs. The weather over the Andes was too poor for flying of this kind and they should not have been forced to press on through it. In one letter to Florence Paton, MP for Rushcliffe in Nottinghamshire, Mary Checklin described one of her very last memories of her son:

'My son's wistful words at the breakfast table on the morning of the 29th [the day of departure] were, "I wish we were not so tired when crossing the Andes." '

In her letter to her MP Mrs Cook said that her husband simply did not have enough experience to do the job asked of him. He shouldn't have been in command, she wrote, not yet. The MPs passed the letters on to the Civil Aviation Ministry. John Booth, chairman of BSAA, was asked by the ministry to respond to the points. He was dismissive. Their hours were not at all excessive and they had been allowed a generous night-stop of seventeen hours before tackling the Andes. As to the weather over the mountains, 'the pilots do in fact always have the final say in such matters', he wrote. 'And no attempt has been made at any time to influence a pilot to undertake a flight against his better judgement.' Finally, on the question of their knowledge of the route, both men were considered to be terribly well qualified, if not necessarily overburdened by experience. 'In view of the comparatively short time the Corporation has been operating this route,' Mr Booth concluded, 'it was inevitable that officers would be flying in the initial stages with less experience than we would desire.'

Florence Paton tried to raise the matter of BSAA's

increasingly dire safety record during a debate in the House of Commons. She was not called by the Speaker to question the government minister. But Mary Checklin should not imagine that her enquiries had been pointless, Florence Paton wrote to her afterwards. 'You may rest assured,' Mrs Paton said, 'that your letter will have its effect in ensuring that other pilots who fly with BSAA will secure proper treatment.'

The implication – that the airline and its pilots would learn something from the rash of accidents they had suffered – was more than just a little optimistic. Already Jack Leche had been in touch again, from the British embassy in Santiago. As with all his letters this one, dated 14 October 1947 and addressed to a Mr Troutbeck at the Foreign Office, was marked 'Personal and Secret'. Leche had recently met the niece of a former colleague, he said, a charming girl called Joanne Jennings Bramley. She had arrived in town aboard an aircraft of BSAA by whom she was employed as a Stargirl. She was, he said, an 'extremely serious and intelligent young woman'. She had even worked for the secret service during the war.

'She told my daughters, who are both working in aviation locally, the younger being employed in the BSAA office, about how sometimes members of air crews had such a hangover that they were hardly fit to fly,' he wrote to Mr Troutbeck, 'and indeed that she had been on several occasions very scared.' It was not the first time that he had encountered a lack of sobriety among BSAA crews, Leche added.

Today most former BSAA pilots deny that drunkenness

was ever a problem among the air crews. Certainly, speaking for themselves, they never drank excessively. After all, they say, Bennett was a teetotaller. He completely disapproved. Who among them would willingly incur his wrath? A few do admit, however, that sometimes a flight departure time would be pulled forward without warning. What had seemed like the innocuous extra tumbler of whisky the night before a long rest day would suddenly become almost the last drink before take-off. But, says Jean Storey – the former Stargirl who, under her maiden name of Jean Fowler, had done so well out of smuggling on the Santiago routes – these were very different times from today. Almost all the men had served during the war. Esprit de corps was everything back then and, more often than not, being a part of the team meant drinking with the team. It was natural that an element of that culture had been carried over into an airline which reflected so many other aspects of the forces' mentality.

'They were never allowed to drink in uniform,' Jean Storey says now of the BSAA air crews. 'But certainly the pilots were used to having an absolute skinful.' They could quite easily feel no ill-effects, she says simply. 'Not like the kids today who are falling down drunk after half a glass of shandy.'

Boozing aside, affairs at BSAA were carrying on much as before: aircraft were still being involved in prangs or near misses and worried diplomats were still firing off secret memos heavy with anxiety. In October 1947 the air attaché at the British embassy in Lima, Peru, Group Captain Pearson, wrote about the airline to the Air Ministry in

London. For eight months of the year Lima sits below a layer of low cloud that smothers the Andean foothills which surround the city. Despite this the North American airlines had managed to maintain a spotless safety record by making sure that no pilot was allowed to bring in an aircraft full of passengers until he had repeatedly served as co-pilot. The same could not be said of BSAA.

'I was extremely surprised,' wrote Group Captain Pearson, 'to discover that the captain of a BSAA aircraft which arrived here some days ago carrying passengers had never been on this route before *at all*. Needless to say he caused the local manager, and the whole Control Tower, some anxious moments breaking cloud.' They had no way of knowing whether he was going to emerge from the cloud-base straight into a hillside. After he emerged safely they still had to stop him from bringing his plane in to land at Las Palmas military airfield to the south, which would not have gone down well with the Peruvian authorities.

A month later, over at Kindley Field airport in Bermuda, the Lancastrian *Starlight*, the very first BSAA aircraft, became the next write-off. On 13 November it took off for the flight to London but soon turned back with engine trouble. It came in too low on its approach and its undercarriage hit a sandbank at the end of the runway. Although nobody was injured, the aircraft was irreparably damaged. The very next day an Avro Tudor IV, the pressurized successor to the York which BSAA had recently brought into service, arrived at Kindley Field from the Azores with what the governor of Bermuda described as 'insufficient fuel safely to complete a single circuit of the airfield'. The emergency services were put on standby as *Star Lion* made its final approach; they were afraid the tanks might finally empty and the engines stutter to a halt before the Tudor had landed. The aircraft, piloted by Cliff Alabaster, made it down safely although that did not satisfy the governor, Admiral Leatham. In a series of tetchy telegrams back to the secretary of state for the colonies in London the admiral claimed that BSAA aircraft were always doing things like this; that the US army, which was the presiding authority at Kindley Field, had complained regularly to their superiors in Washington DC about BSAA aircraft causing mass anxiety because they were either overdue or carrying too little fuel. After investigations by the Air Ministry the governor accepted that it had happened only four times – although that, he said, was four times too many. Alabaster issued his own report on the flight. He said it was a result of hitting unforeseen strong headwinds, nothing more. When they reached the point of no return from the Azores, he said, everything was going according to schedule. They had more than enough fuel to make the trip, but then they hit the weather front and those winds and they had to descend to 2,000 feet to get to calmer conditions.

'There was a Eureka set on board but it wasn't working,' he says today. 'Normally we would have taken sun sights but we were below the cloud. We simply had no way of checking our position. I remember all of us in the cockpit went very quiet. With hindsight we shouldn't have been operating on that route in those conditions.' Weather forecasts, he adds, were often horribly inaccurate.

Something had to give. All along the routes in South

America reports were coming in of aircraft which hadn't been serviced properly or of sloppy repairs being made to engines because of a lack of spares. Late in November 1947 the aviation minister, Lord Nathan, finally asked the Air Safety Board to investigate what was referred to, euphemistically, as the 'operational efficiency' of BSAA. The board requested that Bennett be present when they undertook their investigation. He declined. He wasn't going to hang around while a bunch of petty bureaucrats stuck their noses into the affairs of his airline. He, and only he, was qualified to judge whether it was doing its job properly. He rostered himself on to a service down to South America. 'The Corporation claimed that it was difficult to replace him on the crew roster at short notice,' the Air Safety Board's report said. 'In view of the importance of this enquiry the Board finds difficulty in accepting this as an adequate reason for the absence of the Chief Executive.'

Then the board laid into the airline, albeit in the careful language of Whitehall civil servants. 'The most significant fact emerging from the investigations is the intense desire of the Corporation to pay its way commercially at the earliest possible moment,' the report said. 'The Board has been forced to the conclusion that this aim, highly commendable though it is in principle, has resulted in too intense a drive for economy in certain directions with a consequential tendency to jeopardise the safety of air operations.' It was their way of saying that BSAA was killing passengers in pursuit of profit. Damning though the report was, its recommendations amounted to little more than tinkering around the edges: pilots should have more training, they said. The airline should buy a few more spares. Senior executives of the airline should stop serving as pilots and get on with the job of managing. None of it was going to change the culture of BSAA and, in the close-knit world that Bennett had created, that culture was everything.

Just before Christmas 1947 Air Commodore Vernon Brown, chief inspector of accidents, issued his report on the disappearance of the *Star Dust*, although there really wasn't that much to report on. He listed the service records both of the crew and of the aircraft's components. He described the wind speeds and the cloud cover and the temperatures. There was only one note of criticism in the whole report and that was reserved for Reginald Cook. 'As this was the pilot's first trans-Andean flight in command,' Vernon Brown said, 'and in view of the weather conditions, he should not have crossed by the direct route.' As the earlier exchanges about routes taken by BSAA pilots were top secret Brown would have had no knowledge of them.

Finally under the word 'opinion' he wrote, 'Through lack of evidence due to no wreckage having been found the actual cause of the accident remains obscure. The possibility of severe icing cannot be ignored.' Vernon Brown had looked at the disappearance of the *Star Dust* from every angle. He had pored over every document, considered every statistic, studied every service record. And at the end of all that, he still had no idea what had happened. The *Star Dust* had simply disappeared.

CHAPTER TWENTY

Tupungato, High Andes

2000

REPORTERS NEED SOMETHING TO REPORT. GIVE THEM SILENCE
and they will only attempt to fill it. At the army's base
camp 3,000 metres up Tupungato the silence was deaf-
ening. There was just the wind and the moraine and
the sky. And seventeen very bored journalists, no longer
in the city, not yet on the mountain top. Each and every one
of them was painfully aware that their editors were back in
their offices, waiting for them to file poignant accounts and
television footage of an encounter with a 53-year-old aircraft wreck, complete with human remains. And yet, so far,
nobody had filed anything. It wasn't as if they were stuck
for ways to get their stories out. The army's own satellite
phone was faulty but many of the journalists had their
own. The problem was more basic: they had nothing to
write. They couldn't even turn in a few overwrought para-
graphs on the intimidating challenge of the mountain

because everything had been laid on for them. Here, at base camp, there were lines of field tents and picnic tables. There was a cook and enough wine to keep dinner lubricated. They hadn't had to walk here. Instead they arrived in a convoy of trucks from the Tupungato barracks.

This wasn't what the journalists were after at all. They wanted life-affirming experiences, something with a touch of heroism that would win them a picture by-line. What they had got was a sanitized sightseeing trip to an empty, if attractive, mountainside. What's more, somewhere up above them was the team from the BBC. They had left in the advance party, which included Sergeant Cardozo, a full two days ahead of the rest. God knows what they were doing now. They had the story to themselves.

Standing at base camp when the journalists arrived were around a hundred mules. The mules were there, they were told, for the next stage of the journey. But that next stage would have to wait, Lieutenant Colonel Bustos announced to the expectant journalists, because 'the mules are sleepy'. In a few days they would go. It became clear that the army was waiting for the advance party to finish their part of the job before letting the rest of the press pack anywhere near the site. There were also suggestions that, despite the number of mules already up there, the army had under-estimated the volume of resources needed to keep two expeditions on the mountain.

Only three of the seventeen journalists in the second expedition had any mountaineering experience. Nicolás García was one of them. When he wasn't working at his newspaper, *Los Andes*, he was out climbing the slopes.

That, he always said, was where he was happiest and the prospect of climbing to the wreck of the *Star Dust* rather than spending another week in the office hunched over a word processor had thrilled him. Except it was all turning out to be rather less than thrilling. For García one day at base camp was too many. He asked for permission to go to the crash site by himself. He didn't need an army escort, he said, or even the mules. He could do it by himself.

'I'm in charge of this because the judge put me in charge,' Lieutenant Colonel Bustos barked. 'If anybody disobeys me I will consider him a criminal.' García had his answer. He, like the others, was not happy, and he said so.

This was not what the army had expected. Just days before, on 17 February, Colonel Chretien himself had visited the Tupungato barracks to wish his men well. Over fifty military personnel had been assigned to the operation and they lined up now to take their commanding officer's salute. The drama of the moment was only slightly undermined by Colonel Chretien's mobile phone ringing just as he was about to lift his rigid hand to his rigid brow. He passed the mobile back to a staff officer and made his speech. It was a challenge, he told his men, but one they were more than capable of meeting. Ever the paternalist, he warned them against taking risks with their health on the mountain but informed them that more than enough resources had been made available to get the job done. Finally, he told them that they would be performing their duties before the eyes of the world, in the shape of the international media. It was, he said, a fine opportunity. Now he moved down the line inspecting the men and stopping to shake each one by the hand. When he reached Sergeant Cardozo the colonel paused, reached up and gave him a fatherly pat on the cheek. After all, without Sergeant Cardozo none of this would be happening. The army owed him a debt of gratitude. It would be a terrific expedition.

And yet, just three days later, they were up on the mountain and the journalists were in open revolt.

'The most complicated thing about this whole expedition was managing the journalists,' Lieutenant Colonel Bustos admitted afterwards. 'Rescuing the human remains was easy compared to that. Everybody wanted news for the day whereas our orders were just to make sure that the rescue was conducted properly.'

Starved of anything about the *Star Dust* to report, a number of journalists decided to fill the silence. They filed stories claiming the expedition was stalled due to operational problems; that the army was making a hash of it. Others put it down to sheer inertia on the part of the military. 'This is how things work here,' a British reporter later quoted a lowly army officer as saying. 'The army has an idea and then they realize it is a lot of work – so they decide to wait in the hope everyone gives up and goes home.' But nobody was going anywhere.

Further up the mountain the advance guard had reached the second base camp and was just a day's climbing away from the wreckage. They too were finding the trip less straightforward than they had hoped. Four of their pack animals had been hurt on the long, arduous climb and they now had just enough supplies left for a further forty-eight hours away from base camp. There was no room for error.

The army's reputation depended upon them finding the wreckage the moment they reached the site. Everybody knew there was now a very real chance that, if forced off the mountain by a lack of supplies, they would come down empty-handed. It was a thought few among the party wanted to entertain for too long. What they hadn't anticipated, however, was being beaten to it. How could anybody else slip past them on these battered slopes? They were soldiers of the Eighth Mountain Brigade. Who could be better suited to a job like this than themselves?

The morning of the last full day before they were due to arrive at the site was the same as any other. It was cold, with temperatures down to minus eight degrees Celsius, and the sky was as clear as it had been for much of the expedition. The only sound was the wind across the moraine. Then, quietly at first, came a familiar jagged whirr: a mechanical, man-made sound, alien to this landscape where nature usually has the final say. It became louder and they were forced to look up towards it. Flying low across the slopes were two Lama helicopters, heading towards the furthest reaches of Tupungato. The air force was about to do the unthinkable. They were going to get to the crash site before the army.

The air force had intended to get there days before but they were grounded by poor weather lower down. When they finally did get airborne they were forced to turn back by engine problems on one of the aircraft. (Safety rules demand two helicopters on trips like this so that if one is forced down the other can rescue its crew.) This time, though, everything had gone perfectly. It was Sunday,

20 February and finally Major Estrella was circling just above the crash site, looking down upon the summer-brown slopes and the dirty grey sweep of the glacier and the hordes of *penitentes*. With him he carried a video camera. Carlos Sorini was barred from flying in helicopters due to an old back injury incurred in a plane crash, so he wouldn't be able to view the site for himself. Estrella would get an air-force colleague to record him as he worked his way around the debris field and then together he and Sorini would analyse the tape as best they could. Gently the pilots brought their helicopters in to land.

'I had the impression I was landing on the moon,' Estrella said afterwards. 'Because of the rocks and because you feel like such a small thing against nature.' Very soon he found a piece of a wing's internal framework. They had clearly landed in the right place. Quietly he said a prayer. He did it at every crash site he investigated and there was no good reason to avoid doing it here, regardless of the years that had elapsed. People had still lost their lives here. But time was short. They had no idea when the wind might get up and strand them on the mountain top, ill-equipped to survive the elements. Estrella knew, therefore, that he had to move quickly, or as quickly as the high altitude would allow. But in the video taken that day the major moves anything but quickly. Occasionally he stops moving altogether and simply sits on the slope, panting, trying to get his breath. Towards the end of their short stay on the mountain he starts taking gulps from an oxygen tank. At one point he simply looks up at the clear sky and says, 'We should move faster because the weather could close in,' as though admonishing himself for the physical failings of middle age. It's a vain hope. There's little likelihood of any speed up here, and he knows it.

Estrella works his way across the slope, collecting objects. 'This seems to be a piece of shoe leather,' he says to camera, turning the fragment over in his hands. Soon he is holding a complete man's shoe. It is a white Oxford brogue, although it is not clear whether the leather was originally bleached or if its colour was caused by the elements. 'It was tied,' Estrella says simply. 'So someone was wearing it.' He returns it to the stony ground. Now he picks up a large lump of battered metal. He studies it closely. 'This shows a very strong impact,' he says eventually. 'There's a very great amount of denting caused by a great deceleration.'

Sometimes his comments sound more like the banalities uttered by a tour guide. 'Now we can see to our left a small part of the aeroplane,' he says. Or, 'Here is another part of the wing.' As well as these pieces he also found two huge tyres, each one and a half metres across, one of them still taut with air pressure after half a century. They were only a few metres apart. There was also a major piece of landing gear, relatively undamaged, the propeller that Alejo had seen and the oxygen tanks. Having studied the pattern of debris across the mountainside, Estrella turns to camera and makes a final speech. 'Before leaving this place, as a member of the investigating branch I should announce that we have arrived at the crash site and have an impression of it.' The pieces he had seen suggested an intense impact of some kind, but the debris was scattered across a relatively shallow slope. *Star Dust*, he concludes, had crashed higher up the mountain 'and was brought lower down'.

Just ninety minutes after arriving they were airborne again and on their way back to Mendoza. The supremacy of the air force over the army, which still hadn't reached the crash site, had been secured. Just to be certain everybody knew about it a copy of the video was made, complete with a caption indicating it to be the work of the air force. The tape was given to Cronica, a television news station with studios in Mendoza. That evening they obligingly screened excerpts. The rivalry between the air force and the army had been thrust into the public domain. In a very short time it would be headline news. It would also provide a walk-on part in the story of the *Star Dust* for a former Chilean dictator, even now being held under house arrest many thousands of miles away in Britain, on the edge of an awfully exclusive golf course.

CHAPTER TWENTY-ONE

COLONEL CHRETIEN MISSED THE TELEVISION NEWS THAT Sunday evening. The first thing he knew about it was a telephone call early the next morning from an air-force officer. He took the call in his army apartment on avenida San Martín at 06.00 as he was getting up. The air force had reached the crash site, he was told simply. The army commander thanked the officer for his time and hung up. As he collected his copy of that morning's *Clarín* newspaper, Colonel Chretien could see right away that he had not been the first to know. Thick black headlines declared that the air force had beaten the army to it, and beneath them were large photographs of the crash site complete with wreckage.

'The air force took advantage of the occasion to get themselves into the news,' Colonel Chretien says today. 'Up to that point it was the army that had been all over the newspapers and they wanted to get some of the headlines.'

A little later that morning Colonel Chretien took a second call, this time from General Ricardo Brinzoni, the highest-ranking officer of the Argentinian army, based in Buenos Aires. 'Obviously he was upset by the headlines declaring that the air force had beaten us to it,' Colonel Chretien says. 'He wanted to know whether we were going to continue with our expedition on the mountain or simply abandon it. I told him that our duty was different to that of the air force. Our job was to rescue the remains, which the air force had not done, and that we should continue with it. He agreed.' In any case, the army says now, as Sergeant Cardozo was part of the original expedition which found the wreckage they, and not the air force, were really the first ones to the crash site. And, they add, the army had also been there fifteen years before in 1985, when they brought down the bodies of the climbers Vierio and Rabal. There was nothing really heroic about what the air force had done. They were just playing up to the media.

Shortly after talking to General Brinzoni, Colonel Chretien drove out to the Mendoza air base to see its commander, Colonel Zelaya, and to ask for an explanation. What happened during that meeting has never been revealed but out of it emerged a joint statement. There was no dispute between the two wings of the military, both men said, and the helicopter flights had been entirely complementary to, rather than in conflict with, the army's land expedition. Judge Rodríguez issued his own statement, also declaring that the two services were working together and that he had complete confidence in the way the expedition was proceeding. 'It didn't occur to me to send air force helicopters because I thought they'd have problems dealing with the altitude,' he announced to reporters in Mendoza. 'But then the air accident board made the request [to go up] and I agreed.' It was just that nobody had thought to mention it to the army.

Despite the joint statement there were those in the air force who did not believe their actions had been adequately justified. What were later described as 'sources close to' the air force now set about secretly briefing journalists. According to these off-the-record, deep-background conversations, reported the next day with much wry amusement by parts of the Mendoza press, the air force had had no choice but to get up the mountain as quickly as they could. Reports had been received, they said, that an expedition of Chilean policemen was on its way up to the crash site from the other side of the border. They knew that a King's Messenger had been on board and they wanted to grab his diplomatic bag from among the wreckage because it was believed to contain top secret and highly sensitive documents which could destabilize Argentinian–Chilean relations. The Argentinian air force had made its pre-emptive attack to make sure they got their hands on the all-important diplomatic bag first. All they were doing was serving the best interests of the nation.

Later that day a second, amplified explanation was offered by the same sources, perhaps because the first attempt was so plainly ludicrous, although this new effort was hardly better. In October 1998, while in London for an operation on his back, the former Chilean dictator General

Augusto Pinochet was arrested. A Spanish judge, Baltasar Garzón, had requested the extradition of the general to Madrid for trial on charges of murdering Spanish citizens during his time in power between 1973 and 1990. The Pinochet regime has long been accused of committing state-sponsored murders and of infringing the human rights of hundreds of leftist opponents. Judge Garzón's arrest warrant and request for extradition was one of a number of international attempts to call the general to account, given that he had been granted immunity from prosecution in Chile when he stepped down. The British government had accepted the Spanish request. For more than eighteen months the general had been languishing under house arrest in a modern mansion on the edge of the famous Wentworth golf course just outside London while his lawyers attempted to fight the extradition order all the way up to the highest court in the land, the House of Lords.

The 'sources close to' the air force now said that the real reason the Chilean policemen were trying to get up to the crash site to grab the diplomatic bag was so they could use it as ransom to get the British to release Pinochet. Naturally the Argentinian air force had a duty to confound their dastardly plan. Neither the air force nor the army made any official comment on either version. The premise the stories were based on was false. There was no expedition of Chilean policemen.

But there was an expedition of very bored journalists, still going absolutely nowhere after three days on the mountain's lower slopes. Up at base camp Lieutenant Colonel Bustos received the news by radio of the air force's pre-emptive strike with barely disguised fury. 'They have declared war on us,' he was reported as saying by Caroline Graham of the British newspaper, the *Mail on Sunday*. 'If we have to crawl there on our hands and knees and we have to die doing it, I have been told I have to get you to the site.' The reputation of the army depended upon it. The second party was finally on the move.

From the base camp to the next camp was an arduous trek of at least ten hours which would take them up over the Azufre high pass at 4,800 metres. They set off early with the inexperienced climbers on the less-loaded mules at the front and the more experienced on the heavily loaded mules at the back. It did not take long for the groups to become separated along the mountain paths and for the overburdened animals to start bucking and kicking at the heavy demands being made upon them. By the end of the journey at least two of the mules had fallen down the side of the mountain, taking some of the journalists' expensive equipment with them, and one soldier had broken his leg in two places. He had to be accompanied back down by a number of his comrades. Further up the mountain Sergeant Cardozo's advance army expedition was experiencing its own problems. One of its men had been taken ill with a suspected pulmonary oedema, a potentially fatal condition in which fluid gathers on the lung as a result of exposure to high altitude. He had to be pulled off the slopes, his arms about the shoulders of two fellow climbers so that his feet left furrows in the moraine where his listless toes had dragged. At the request of the army the air force agreed to return to Tupungato and helicopter him off.

The journalists now had something tangible to report and, to the fury of some of the officers, they did so with great enthusiasm. Lost mules, injured soldiers and air rescues all had the hallmark of a real story. It was also the only story on offer: when they reached the high altitude camp, where the advance party had been based for days, it was deserted. Sergeant Cardozo, the BBC camera crew and the other soldiers were at the crash site gathering up the human remains. The journalists demanded to be allowed up there but Lieutenant Colonel Bustos refused. The remains would be collected first, as the judge's orders demanded, and then they would be brought down to this camp where a press conference would be held. That was when they could get their photographs, he said.

The cameraman Miguel Moreno y Gil, who was not used to having his stories stage-managed, stood smoking his black cigarettes and shaking his head. As far as he was concerned this was not journalism. 'If I want to shoot a movie,' he said between drags, 'I go to Hollywood where the women are better.' (Moreno was killed two months later by a sniper's bullet while covering the civil war in Sierra Leone. He was just thirty-two years old.) But Moreno, like the others, had no choice. He had to do as the army said.

Later that day the advance party came down from the crash site, carrying the human body parts in large black plastic bin bags. Khaki groundsheets were laid out on the dusty ground and on top of them was laid a set of white sheets to add a clinical backdrop to the proceedings. The Air Accident Investigation Board had asked the army to allow a doctor, climber and pilot called Carlos Bauzá to accompany them on the advance party so he could examine the wreckage and the remains in situ. Now he knelt down on the groundsheets and prepared to remove the pieces from the bin bags. Before he could continue Lieutenant Colonel Bustos made an announcement.

'The media should be respectful,' he said. 'I think there should be praying.'

The journalists did as they were told. They had learnt that it was the only way to get anything on this expedition. Yet again words of piety and devotion were muttered over the remains of the long departed. Once they had observed a minute's silence Lieutenant Colonel Bustos declared himself satisfied. They could begin.

Carlos Bauzá removed the body parts one by one from the bin bags. 'This a humerus,' he said holding up a piece of a limb, 'and this is a fibula.' The photographers snapped away furiously. There was a piece of coccyx bone, and a man's hand holding just a single digit. There was a torso and that slender female hand that Sergeant Cardozo had seen the first time he arrived at the crash site, its fingers curling up together. In all Carlos Bauzá believed they had recovered the remains of four people. When they had been photographed they were placed in leather carrying cases for the long journey by mule back down the mountain. For a dozen of the journalists that was the end of their expedition. They believed they had the best material they were likely to get. An arduous climb to the crash site wasn't going to give them anything else other than leg ache and altitude sickness. They decided to follow the body parts as they descended first to base camp and then on to the Tupungato barracks.

The remaining half-dozen journalists, including Nicolás García, climbed onwards to the crash site where they pitched their tents for the night. As the sun was setting García went for a walk. As with everybody else who had been there he soon found wreckage: the shoes and wallets, the fragments of clothes and pieces of wing. He came across a roll of old 35mm cine film, still tightly coiled. He picked it up and squinted at a frame through the fast-falling light. It was some old movie, part of the cargo listed on the manifest. There was an elegant woman in the frame with her platinum blonde hair stacked high. She wore a bustier and a feather boa about her neck and there was a look of wry amusement on her face, perhaps at some comment made by her companion, a gentleman in a tightly fitted double-breasted suit who wore his hair carefully slicked back. It was, literally, a snapshot from another age; the age in which the passengers of the *Star Dust* had lived and breathed. 'I suddenly realized that I was standing where people had died,' García says. 'I was in a graveyard. And I began to wonder why we had made all the effort to get here.'

Back down at the Tupungato barracks both the defence attaché and the press attaché of the British embassy were waiting to meet the rest of the expedition. Just to make sure the body parts had been adequately prayed over, the Lord's prayer was now recited in Spanish and English. Finally Colonel Hammond Massey, the defence attaché, thanked the army for their efforts in carrying out what was later described by the embassy as a 'macabre and thankless task'.

Within days the remains were in a laboratory in Buenos

Aires. Over the next few weeks blood samples were gathered from those relatives who had come forward and they too were dispatched to the Argentinian capital. In a couple of months, they were told, it should be possible using modern DNA testing methods to identify which body parts belonged to which crew member or passenger. Then they could be returned for burial. The scientists went to work.

CHAPTER TWENTY-TWO

IT WAS A BUMPY, TIRESOME RIDE FROM THE START. SHORTLY after leaving London for Lisbon on the morning of 28 January 1948, *Star Tiger* developed both engine trouble and a fault on the gyrocompass. Then the heater failed. The heaters on these Tudor IVs were always failing, filling the cabin with condensation so that a cold rain fell on the passengers. The cabin crew were constantly having to go back into the cabin mid-flight and lift up the floorboards to get the thing working. It made the new aircraft's pressurization an irrelevance. If the heater failed the crew had to take the aircraft right down from its cruising altitude of 20,000 feet to around 2,000 feet so that the passengers didn't freeze to death. There were also recurring problems with the Tudor's hydraulics and some of the wiring. Of course Don Bennett wouldn't hear a word against it. The aircraft was British. It was made by A.V. Roe. It was irrelevant that BOAC had refused to operate them. That just proved what a disreputable outfit the so-called competition was. It was a fine piece of kit and Bennett would defend it all the way. His career, like too many of his passengers, would suffer as a result.

Star Tiger departed Lisbon for the Azores over two hours late and, despite repairs on the ground, the heater was soon failing once more. According to the schedule it should have taken off again from Santa Maria in the Azores for Bermuda that evening so as to use the starry night skies for navigation, but it didn't. Waiting on the island was a BSAA Lancastrian carrying spares and other freight down to Bermuda. Together the pilots of the two aircraft – Captain Brian McMillan in the Tudor, Captain Frank Griffin in the Lancastrian, both of whom were former Pathfinders – studied the weather reports. They predicted strong head winds across the remaining Atlantic stretch and both men decided to delay for twenty-four hours. The next afternoon at 15.34 *Star Tiger* took off for the 1,981-nautical-mile journey. She was overloaded by around a thousand pounds. There were thirty-one people on board: its crew of four, two Stargirls and twenty-five passengers, including Air Marshal Sir Arthur Coningham – one of the architects of Britain's air war.

The Lancastrian was out ahead by about an hour and during the night the two aircraft kept in touch with each other by radio, the leading plane letting *Star Tiger* know that the winds were stronger than expected. McMillan announced he would keep *Star Tiger* down at 2,000 feet where the winds should have been lighter, although that caused problems of its own. It meant flying below the cloud where there would be no hope of an astro-fix for the navigator. With no access to radio beacons on the route until the last few hundred miles, the crew would be plotting their route from the compass and wind measurements alone. Still, as far as the Lancastrian could tell, everything seemed to be going according to plan. Only one thing was odd: whenever *Star Tiger*'s radio officer sent forward a message he stated the plane's cruising altitude as 20,000 feet instead of 2,000. Perhaps it was a mistake, a slip of the finger on the Morse code key.

At 03.15 on 30 January 1948 the Tudor took its bearings from the radio operator in Bermuda. The island should then have been only a short distance away. That was the last anybody ever heard of the aircraft. All attempts to raise it on the radio were met only with the rush and whistle of static. Within twenty-five minutes the alarm had been raised and a number of aircraft, including Frank Griffin's Lancastrian, set out to scour the area around where *Star Tiger* had last been heard from, but there was nothing: no wreckage, no bodies, not even a slick of oil. It had gone and so had its thirty-one passengers and crew.

Other BSAA pilots could only guess at what had happened. Perhaps Captain McMillan really had thought he was flying at 20,000 feet when he was only at 2,000 feet. It had been a long, troublesome flight and he could have been tired. As he descended he would have slammed into the sea at full speed and the aircraft would have disintegrated immediately. Perhaps there was some vital mechanical failure. Perhaps the heating system had exploded.

Back in London the Air Registration Board asked for a meeting with the aviation minister, Lord Nathan. In view of the disappearance, they said, it would be better if all Tudor IVs were grounded until the cause of the crash had been identified. Lord Nathan agreed. On 2 February he informed Bennett by telephone.

BSAA's chief executive was furious. 'Is the ARB withdrawing the certificate of airworthiness?' Bennett asked. 'That's the only legal way in which an aircraft can be grounded.'

Lord Nathan said no, the certificate had not been withdrawn, 'in the absence of positive evidence to justify it. Meanwhile, pending the results of the investigation, the ARB has advised that it might be prudent to ground the aircraft.'

Now Bennett exploded. 'The accident is serious enough but this is unbelievable,' he said. 'I know there are many who don't like my outspoken ways but this is well beyond anything I have ever contemplated.' It would destroy British aviation for years to come, he said. Bennett was being overdramatic, Lord Nathan replied. In any case that was his decision. All BSAA services using Tudor IVs should be cancelled immediately. Bennett pleaded with him. They would lose money. The minister ignored him.

The next day the deputy chairman of BSAA, Sir John Stephenson, called the minister to plead with him. 'BSAA might as well close down,' Sir John said. 'The resignation of the whole board might follow.'

Lord Nathan was unimpressed. 'I don't see why,' he said. And then he added, 'It is a serious decision and I realize the repercussions.' But there it is. He had taken expert advice.

Bennett was still seething. He contacted the *Daily Express*, then the biggest-selling newspaper in Britain, and gave an interview. It appeared on 5 February as a single running statement under the headline 'I contest Lord Nathan's grounding of Tudor IV'. As chief executive of a state-owned corporation Bennett was, essentially, attacking his ultimate boss. And he was doing it very publicly.

Civil aviation, he announced, had become a political football, subject to endless meddling by those either in it to make a fast buck or who were simply 'anti-British'. 'Interference with management has now reached such a degree that it has become increasingly difficult for an air-line to be held responsible for the results it achieves.' He had total faith in the mighty Tudor IV, he said. 'Every investigation and precaution has been carried out with it,' he said. 'Training of crews handling the Tudor IV has been meticulously executed and the crews have been checked. That we should have lost a Tudor IV in spite of all this is as unbelievable as the circumstances of the accident themselves.' The decision to ground it should have been his and his alone.

Later that day an emergency meeting was convened between Lord Nathan and his most senior advisers on one side and Sir John Stephenson of BSAA on the other. After informing Sir John that he was receiving an increasing number of complaints about BSAA's safety record Lord Nathan turned his attention to the article. It was appalling for a man in Bennett's position to have done such a thing, he said. What's more it was not the first time he had behaved like this. Bennett was constantly attacking the ministry in the pages of leading aviation journals. It just wasn't on. Sir John agreed. Bennett had given no warning that he was about to talk to the *Daily Express*. There was even a board meeting the night before, a stormy one with Bennett throwing rages and then falling into deep brooding silences. He could have informed them then of what he intended to do but he didn't. The first the board of directors knew about it was when they picked up their morning papers.

'The article was gravely improper to say the least,' Sir John said finally.

Lord Nathan accepted his assurances that the article was the result of Bennett acting alone and asked Sir John what he was going to do about it. The BSAA director begged for a few days' breathing space. He needed to talk it over with Sir John Booth, chairman of BSAA, and he would not be available until the weekend. Lord Nathan agreed.

On 6 February Bennett contacted Lord Nathan's office and asked for a face-to-face meeting. There was a confidential matter he needed to discuss, he said. He was rebuffed. The minister didn't want to see him until the senior board members of BSAA had discussed their own tactics. Instead Bennett wrote to him. The letter was headed 'secret' and began with a suddenly emollient, almost affectionate address:

My dear Minister,

Obviously the most likely cause of the loss of STAR
TIGER is sabotage. After preliminary discussions with

197

members of M.I.5. [the British secret intelligence service] we felt that there was a very good cause for investigating possible criminal aspects of the loss of this British aircraft. M.I.5. were apparently themselves anxious to help but we have since been informed that it is not within their terms of reference. They did, however, on my behalf, contact C.I.D. [Criminal Investigations Department of the police] to request their assistance in this matter. I am now informed by M.I.5. that C.I.D. have refused to co-operate.

I wonder whether there was anything which you might do to help.

Yours sincerely,

D.C.T. Bennett

The request was pointedly ignored and dismissed within the ministry as evidence of 'a lack of perspective' by Bennett over the affair. Nevertheless he kept to his sabotage theory for the rest of his life, even though there was not a scintilla of evidence to support it. He claimed that a well-known Second World War saboteur had been sighted near *Star Tiger* when it was on the airfield at Santa Maria in the Azores. The saboteur had been employed, he said, by representatives of the powerful North American airlines who wanted to knock BSAA out of the market so they could have the lucrative South American and Caribbean trade routes to themselves. With the help of friends in the intelligence services Bennett believed he had almost completed his own investigations when, he claimed, the prime minister, Clement Attlee, intervened. The enquiries into this matter had to cease, Bennett said he was informed, because it would imperil international relations. Again there is not a single piece of evidence to back up Bennett's version of events. It may simply have been easier for him to imagine both himself and his airline, which genuinely had been at the centre of a fierce trade war, to be the victims of some ghastly plot rather than of a clumsy aircraft's mechanical failure.

On 9 February there was another meeting in Lord Nathan's office, this time attended by both Sir John Booth and Sir John Stephenson. They immediately offered to resign. They had already tried asking Bennett to quit and he had refused so they were left with no option. The board could not work with the man, not after his repeated disloyalties. They had been planning to have a showdown with him even before the *Daily Express* article. Time and again he had ignored the board and gone his own way. As to the safety of BSAA, 'Bennett always has a plausible answer to any doubts expressed by the board of any particular project,' Sir John Booth said. 'But his record condemns him.'

Lord Nathan listened carefully. He understood what they were saying. It was him or them and if Bennett wouldn't resign then they had to. The minister had a better idea: sack Bennett. Later BSAA claimed that the decision to get rid of their founding chief executive was all the board's own work, that there was no influence from government and that politicians had not been involved. Minutes of the secret meetings that were held during February 1948 make it clear that nothing could be further from the truth. It was

Lord Nathan who first suggested getting rid of Bennett and Lord Nathan who wanted him to go with the very minimum pay-off.

'You must take legal advice,' Lord Nathan said, 'so as to make sure Bennett has no grounds to claim wrongful dismissal.'

The BSAA executives proposed giving him a generous severance package equivalent to a year's pay. They were sure he would go quietly with that in his pocket.

'I think three months', in the circumstances, would be adequate in this case,' Lord Nathan said. 'Normally misconduct would not involve payment on dismissal at all. And there's no doubt that the *Daily Express* article is misconduct.'

For the moment the men settled on a compromise: a pay-off of six months' wages. Now Lord Nathan returned to an earlier proposition, as if it were an itch that needed constant scratching. 'Are you sure we can't get him to resign?' the minister said. 'Then we won't have to pay him off at all.'

'He won't resign,' Sir John Booth said. 'He would regard it as tantamount to an admission of having failed in the discharge of his duties.'

Lord Nathan accepted what he had been told. They would have to sack him and they would have to pay him to go. Don Bennett's career was about to become the thirty-second victim of the disappearance of *Star Tiger*. He just didn't know it yet.

CHAPTER TWENTY-THREE

QUIETLY LORD NATHAN'S DOGGED CIVIL SERVANTS BEGAN their labours, examining every facet of Don Bennett's time at BSAA. There was little doubt in anybody's mind: the man had sacked himself. Still, nothing was being left to chance. If he tried to come back and argue his corner – and nobody would put it past him – the ministry wanted to make sure they had chapter and verse on every single mis-demeanour and safety violation, every gaffe and cock-up. The document they produced was marked 'confidential', ran to over twenty-six pages of tightly packed foolscap and was headed simply 'Note on Air Vice-Marshal Bennett's Record as Chief Executive of BSAA'.

Much of it was obvious. There were the crashes, and the occasions when he had caused diplomatic incidents by wading into delicate negotiations in Uruguay or Brazil. There was his attitude to the ministry and his lax management style. There were his political outbursts. At the end of May 1947, the document reported, Bennett attended a Liberal Party rally where he gave a speech. 'We fought a war for freedom against some people calling themselves National Socialists,' he told the mob, 'then we turn around and elect people with the same ideas to govern the country.' Comparing the policies of the British government, who were his employers, to those of the Nazi party was not a way to win friends.

The power of this secret memo lay not so much in its detail as in its comprehensiveness. Most of this material had already been recorded by the ministry, of course, but it lay in different files and on different desks. Nobody had thought to make a connection between his brusque, gung-ho approach to matters of government regulation and how he might behave towards his own pilots. Nobody had thought to identify a pattern. After years of appeasing Bennett, mostly because of his war record, here, finally, was the full story.

On 10 February Lord Nathan wrote to Clement Attlee detailing the case and its endgame, which was fast approaching. By now Lord Nathan had accepted that the only way to assure a modest amount of cooperation from Bennett was to line his pockets. 'A gratuitous payment will be made to him of £4,500,' he told the prime minister, 'which is equivalent of a year's salary.' That same day the secretary to the board of BSAA wrote to Bennett informing him that he had lost their confidence as a result of the *Daily Express* article. They had therefore decided to 'terminate your appointment as Chief Executive'. Although he was not entitled to any cash, they had decided to send him a cheque in the sum of £4,580 11 shillings and 8 pence, being both discretionary severance pay of £4,500 and any outstanding wages. A terse statement containing only the information that Bennett had been sacked was released to the press. Bennett responded in his own inimitable style. He had a long-standing engagement to give a speech that evening at Oxford University's Cosmos Society. 'I warn you never be successful,' he told the assembled students and dons. 'You will suffer enormously. Today I have had the proudest honour of my life conferred on me. I have been sacked for having spoken my mind.'

Clearly Bennett didn't feel he had said enough. A parliamentary by-election was pending in Croydon, to the south of London, and he managed to get himself adopted as the Liberal Party candidate. During the campaign he declared that, under Clement Attlee's Labour government, the British people had been thrust into 'a state of servitude, of restrictions and a spiritual poverty unbelievable in this land of freedom'. It didn't make much of an impression on the voters. He came last in the election and lost his deposit.

Over in the Civil Aviation Ministry a file had been opened entitled 'A.V.M. Bennett: termination of services as chief executive of BSAA'. Inside the manila folder, registration number BT 217/2036, was recorded every twist and turn in the affair. Now that affair was at an end. Bennett was not questioning his dismissal. It was time to send the documents for storage at the Public Record Office. Under what is known as the thirty-year rule officials have the power to mark a file closed to the public if its contents are considered in any way politically or personally sensitive. If a file relates to internal government business it is almost always marked closed in this way, usually – as the name of the rule suggests – for thirty years. But those officials do have the discretion to close a file for very much longer if they see fit. It is a mark of Bennett's standing that his file was deemed to be a suitable case for such treatment. It dealt with the personal affairs and character failings of one man, a famous war hero. As the former commander of the Pathfinders he warranted at least a modicum of respect. The civil servant decreed that it should be closed for a full seventy-five years. It could not be opened to the public until 2024, when all the key players in the drama would be dead.

In recent years the British government has proclaimed a policy of greater openness. Decisions on the closure of files can now be challenged. After just such an appeal the government considered the contents of file BT 217/2036 in detail. For good or ill Bennett had all but been forgotten. Today his military record is just a footnote in the history of Britain's war effort, bleakly overshadowed by that of Bomber Harris. The government decided the seventy-five-year rule need no longer apply. The file was opened twenty-four years ahead of time, specifically for the purposes of this book.

At the same time as the file was being closed and sent for storage, Bennett's loyal former staff at BSAA were trying to come to terms with his departure. Some of them had distinctly mixed feelings. 'There was a sense of inevitability about Bennett's going,' Cliff Alabaster says today. 'And a sense that we had all been let down. We were most of us inexperienced in civil aviation and he was a very forceful man. I think one could fairly say that he pushed things to the limit with people who were relying on him for direction.' In the end, for all his bluff and bluster and certainty, the great navigator simply did not know how to provide his staff with direction.

If Bennett had so wished he could doubtless have found ways to convince himself that his airline's troubles were just something that came with the territory rather than anything to do with him. After his sacking there were still crashes and there were still fatalities. On 5 January 1949 the York *Star Venture* (which had flown the Dakar–Buenos Aires leg of the ill-fated service CS59 of which *Star Dust* was a part) crashed into a mangrove swamp four hundred miles north of Rio, its wings trailing ribbons of flame through the dark night sky. Three of the nine passengers were killed and the pilot broke his ankle. (The counterargument would, of course, have been the endurance of the culture instilled into the airline by Bennett.)

Bennett was also able to take comfort from the findings of the MacMillan enquiry into the loss of *Star Tiger* – or, to be exact, the lack of findings. According to Lord MacMillan there were 'no grounds for supposing that *Star Tiger* fell into the sea in consequence of having been deprived of her radio, having failed to find her destination, and having exhausted her fuel'. Whatever event had caused her disappearance it had been exceptionally rapid because there had been no distress signal, or at least none that had been picked up by any of the nearby radio stations. 'In closing this report it may truly be said that no more baffling case has ever been presented for investigation,' the noble lord wrote. All they could do, he said, was speculate that somewhere, in the complex relationship between man and machine which governs safe aviation, something cataclysmic had occurred. 'What happened in this case will never be known,' Lord MacMillan concluded, 'and the fate of *Star Tiger* must forever remain an unsolved mystery.' Bennett was vindicated. Nobody had been able to prove that there was anything wrong with the Tudor. He might not be at BSAA but at least the company's Tudors were back in service.

Soon the mystery of *Star Tiger* was joined by another. On 17 January 1949 thirteen passengers boarded the Tudor *Star Ariel*, under the command of Captain McPhee, for the five-hour flight to Kingston, Jamaica. An hour into the flight McPhee sent back a routine message: he was at 18,000 feet and visibility was good. After one more short, routine message there was only silence. There was no distress signal and certainly no reports of a crash. Other aircraft were dispatched to comb the area from the skies but again, as with *Star Tiger*, there was nothing: just clear skies above and the deep blue seas of the Caribbean below. American ships that criss-crossed the stretch of water she had last been flying over found only the lonely horizon. The Tudor was lost and with it had gone her thirteen passengers and seven crew.

In the years that followed, the disappearances of both *Star Tiger* and *Star Ariel* became the subject of endless speculation by aficionados of the so-called Bermuda Triangle, the stretch of the Atlantic famed for swallowing up ships and aircraft, which both were flying over when they vanished. The two BSAA aircraft appear regularly in articles about the triangle published in magazines (and their Internet equivalents) dedicated to the study of Unidentified Flying Objects (UFOs). In these accounts the Tudors' vanishing is easily explained. They were spirited away by flying saucers and snatched, not just out of mid-air, but out of the entire solar system.

The immediate impact of *Star Ariel*'s loss was rather more down to earth, literally. All the passenger-carrying Tudors were grounded again and BSAA had to get by on its ever-diminishing fleet of tired old Yorks and Lancastrians. Eventually, after months of fruitless investigation, the Air Registration Board ruled that, having failed to establish why the two aircraft disappeared, it could not recommend the renewal of the certificates of airworthiness on the Tudors. For BSAA it was the end of the road. After Bennett's generally successful attempts to keep the airline in profit it was now losing many thousands of pounds a month. Throughout early 1949 losses climbed towards the million-pound mark. Without the Tudors there was simply no way of turning the company around. The Yorks and Lancastrians – those that were still in service – were not up to the job. Lord Nathan had been replaced at the Civil Aviation Ministry by Francis Pakenham. He now recognized that BSAA was no longer a viable company. By the Airways Corporation Act of July 1949, the entirety of BSAA was taken over by BOAC. Almost five years before, BOAC had argued that it should be given responsibility for the South American routes. Now, without having to lift a finger, it had won the prize.

Many of BSAA's employees simply swapped over to the old enemy. 'There was a certain amount of trepidation about it,' says former BSAA pilot Don Mackintosh today. 'Mind you, with all the crashes that had happened it wasn't really a surprise. Frankly, I think we were grateful to still have a job.'

Of the thirty-six passenger-carrying aircraft owned and operated by BSAA between January 1946 and July 1949, at least ten were destroyed in crashes. Four of those crashed aircraft were from among the six original Lancastrians with which the company started operations. One of those was the *Star Dust*. A total of ninety-six people lost their lives: seventy-four passengers and twenty-two BSAA employees.

By today's standards, when a single air crash can all too easily take with it the lives of hundreds of people, the over-all tally may not look too desperate. But BSAA's statistics are from the earliest days of commercial long-haul flight and its passengers were pioneers. Back then individual air-craft rarely carried more than a dozen passengers at a time, and more often, as with the *Star Dust*, just half that number. Services didn't leave five or ten times daily but twice a week at the most. It is likely that the average number of passengers who pass through Heathrow every day at the beginning of the twenty-first century – more than 175,000 – is greater than the number which passed through the same airport every *year* in the 1940s. Air travel was a rare luxury reserved only for the well-heeled and the im-portant. It was they who were the victims of Don Bennett's Bomber Command in mufti.

CHAPTER TWENTY-FOUR

Mendoza

2000

ONE MORNING DURING HIS STAY IN MENDOZA CARLOS SORINI went to a toy shop in the city and bought a model kit for a Lancaster bomber. He had wanted a Lancastrian but the shop didn't have any of those. There wasn't much call for models of Avro Lancastrians in Mendoza. The old Lancaster would have to do. Back at their temporary office on the air-force base Sorini and Major Luis Estrella put the model together, like two schoolboys dreaming of grand adventures in the skies. Just as A.V. Roe had done to create the original Lancastrian, Luis Estrella reshaped the nose. He altered the tail and covered over the gun turret on its spine. Finally he painted it silver. Their powerful lap-top computers with their weather-modelling software and detailed satellite maps were all fine sophisticated tools for air-crash investigations but they were no substitute for a model like this: a three-dimensional visual reference for the kind of aircraft whose shattered remains they were investigating. It helped every now and then to be able to pick up the model and study it; to turn it over in their hands and imagine it in flight, bucking and bouncing through heavy turbulence over the mountains.

In any case, if they were going to have any hope of finding out why the *Star Dust* crashed they needed all the help they could get. 'Normally the first thing we do after there has been a crash is we walk around the site,' Carlos Sorini says. 'We take photographs. We make a map. We look for witnesses. We take notes to describe the crash zone.' However, that methodology relies on the investigators arriving at the crash scene as soon after the impact as possible. Usually that means a matter of hours rather than days. 'If you don't arrive at the time you should arrive,' Sorini says, 'everything changes.'

Nothing could have changed more than the *Star Dust* crash site. The wreckage had almost certainly shifted from the original point of impact. They knew too that the slope of Tupungato where the fragments had been uncovered was a good fifty miles away from where the radio officer, Denis Harmer, had claimed they were, just minutes off a supposed landing at Santiago. Not only that, Tupungato was well off the route the *Star Dust* was supposed to have been taking. Normally BSAA's Lancastrians crossed on a reasonably direct east to west route over Mendoza that took them above a mountain pass close to Aconcagua. Then, once clear of the Andes, they would turn due south for the run into Santiago. The position of the wreckage on Tupungato, south of Aconcagua, only makes sense if at Mendoza

Reginald Cook put his aircraft on a south-westerly heading. That would have taken him on the shorter – and deeply unorthodox – diagonal path straight over the peaks and down into the Chilean capital. Perhaps he felt the Lancastrian's ability to fly at high altitude meant his aircraft could simply clear the mountains. It did at least tally with the disclosure that BSAA's station manager in Buenos Aires, Wing Commander Trevor Waymouth, made back in August 1947 to the British air attaché. Waymouth had admitted that BSAA pilots might sometimes put in a flight plan for the direct route and then take another route entirely, although the wing commander had claimed the errant pilots only went north, rather than south as Cook clearly had.

Nevertheless, that might explain *where* the wreckage had been found. It did not answer the other big question: *why* did the *Star Dust* crash? During his time at the crash site Carlos Bauzá, the doctor and climber working with the AAIB, logged every single piece of wreckage he and the soldiers found, using a hand-held global positioning system. By transferring the coordinates to a computerized, three-dimensional map of the area, those fragments could then be placed exactly on the mountainside. It provided a detailed picture of the debris field's shape. Every debris field tells a story and to Bauzá this one was clear even before he left the mountain. It was also obvious to the other investigators when they saw it on the computer screen.

Both in 1947, when the *Star Dust* disappeared, and in January 2000, when Sergeant Cardozo and the Moisos found it, one theory had kept coming up time and again:

that the aircraft was brought down by sabotage. A King's Messenger was on board. Relations between Argentina and Britain were notoriously bad. Perhaps the messenger was carrying documents to Chile which Juan Domingo Perón did not wish the authorities in Santiago to receive. A bomb, timed to explode over the mountains, would deal efficiently with the problem.

The debris field immediately ruled out that possibility. When an aircraft explodes in mid-air the wreckage is spread over dozens of square miles. It is picked up on the wind and thrown off in all directions. (After Pan Am's flight 103 was blown out of the sky by a terrorist bomb over the Scottish town of Lockerbie in 1988, the debris was scattered over an area of 845 square miles.) On Tupungato the debris was scattered over an area of just one square mile, no more and possibly a little less. This was not the result of a mid-air explosion.

The debris also ruled out one other possibility: a sharp nosedive vertically into the ground due to a sudden stall. If that happens the wreckage is very concentrated. Its heart can be measured in square metres rather than square miles. Even after fifty-three years they could see that this was not the wreckage of a stalled aircraft. The *Star Dust* had crashed for some other reason and in some other way.

They turned their attention to the bleached pieces of wreckage that both Bauzá and Estrella had seen during their separate trips to the site. 'Every piece of wreckage was very important,' Sorini says, 'because it too tells us a story. For example, when we looked at the main landing gear we could see it was in a good condition.' The two tyres were also remarkably intact. One of them even contained air and they were lying close to each other. 'This told us that the landing gear was still up when *Star Dust* crashed, not down.' If it had been down at the moment of impact, in preparation for touchdown, the landing gear and the tyres would have been ripped to pieces. The crew was definitely not preparing the aircraft for any kind of emergency landing. And then there was the propeller that Alejo Moiso had first found on the mountain. Its tips were scarred and turned back on themselves. That kind of damage was familiar to all the investigators. It meant the engines were working and their propellers turning at the moment of impact. The Lancastrian was flying normally.

'In modern terminology what happened to the aircraft is known as a CFIT,' says Sorini. 'It means controlled flight into terrain.' It suggests the BSAA crew had no sense they were about to crash.

There was one other major factor that the team now needed to consider: the weather. There is no doubt that the conditions over the mountains were appalling on 2 August 1947. It was ill-advised for Cook to attempt a crossing even in an aircraft like the Lancastrian capable of relatively high altitudes. Looking now at old maps and statistics held in the archives of the Argentinian weather service, Sorini and Estrella could quickly see something that was vital. The crew of the *Star Dust* had been flying into a weather phenomenon about which they knew nothing.

Then again, by 1947 very few other people in aviation knew anything about it either. The first hint of its existence came only in the winter of 1944, far over on the other side of the world from where Cook was flying. That November almost a hundred B–29 Superfortress bombers set out from US air bases in the Pacific for the first bombing raids on Tokyo. The B–29 was a substantial aircraft that could reach altitudes of over 30,000 feet, which was where the pilots chose to fly during this mission. As they approached the target area the aircraft turned east over Mount Fuji to begin their bombing run. Suddenly they found themselves accelerating up to speeds of 450 miles per hour. It was a good 90 miles faster than the B–29 was supposed to be capable of and the intended targets flashed by beneath them. Unable to recalibrate their targeting in time, the vast majority of the bombs were dropped far off the mark. The raid was, militarily, a dismal failure, but it provided meteorologists with something to ponder. It seemed that at the altitudes the bombers were flying some kind of fierce wind was pushing them along.

Immediately after the war intense research began, with weather balloons and high-altitude aircraft measuring wind speeds in the upper atmosphere. It was the University of Chicago which, in 1947, announced the discovery of the 'jet stream': a great current of brutal wind in a wide ribbon a couple of miles deep which would certainly be found above 20,000 feet where *Star Dust* was flying. The research, though, was in progress – it would not reach maturity for a further ten years – and the pilots of BSAA were not privy to it. Some jet streams were recorded where temperate air masses met the tropics. Others appeared where polar air masses met temperate air. All of them were dependent on specific temperature and air-pressure conditions, combined with the earth's rotation. They could blow at as little as 60 miles per hour and as much as 290. And if in 1947 you were flying into one and didn't know it, any attempt to plot your route would be more or less useless.

Looking at the weather statistics for 2 August 1947 the investigators could see that the atmospheric conditions were perfect for the formation of a jet stream along the route the *Star Dust* was following. They flew head-on into it. Making judgements based upon the air speed they were recording in the cockpit and the time that had elapsed, the crew of the *Star Dust* would have presumed that they had cleared the mountains; that below the cloud was the fine city of Santiago. And so they began to descend, completely unaware that they were heading directly for the sheer eastern face of Tupungato.

Some of BSAA's pilots have expressed scepticism at the investigators' conclusions. 'I really don't think Reginald Cook would have started his descent,' Cliff Alabaster says, 'unless he had a positive indication that he'd crossed the mountains.' He also says that, while it's true they didn't know about something called the jet stream, they were well aware of very strong winds over the Andes. 'I remember on one flight across the Andes we encountered this severe downdraught,' he says. 'It was as if this bloody great hammer had hit us. And when we landed at Santiago there was distinct damage to the wing tips.'

Another former BSAA pilot, Jeff Rees, had a similar experience. 'We were on full climb power over the Andes and even so we were descending at a rate of 500 feet per minute because of the head wind. Luckily I was able to turn around and head south to cross down there. But if Reginald Cook caught the wind later in the flight perhaps he didn't have a chance to turn around.' As far as Rees is concerned the suggestion that the crew had no way of knowing about the weather conditions which were delaying them is unproven. But, he accepts, it is most likely that strong winds were in some way the cause.

We can only guess at what the eleven passengers and crew experienced in those last few moments of their flight, if Bauzá, Sorini and Estrella's version of the crash is correct. Would they have been concerned about the level of turbulence they were experiencing as they bounced and rocked across the Andes? Certainly the crew would have given a damn. None of them liked severe turbulence. It meant they had less control of the flight than they wanted; that the weather was dictating the aircraft's movements, not the engines. But the passengers probably wouldn't have been much alarmed. Commercial aviation of this sort was still very much in its infancy and most passengers expected a bumpy ride. After all it was pioneering stuff. If they were in any doubt about the drama of what they were doing they needed only to look up at the tube that was delivering them oxygen and keeping them alive.

As to the impact, it's unlikely they knew anything about it. Even if they had survived the crash – a remote possibility – they would suddenly have been exposed to the low oxygen atmosphere and then blacked out. After that the investigators believe the crash triggered an avalanche which smothered the wreckage and hid it from view. That was why the search parties found nothing in 1947; there was simply nothing to find.

'The passengers would not have realized at any moment what was happening,' says Carlos Bauzá. 'I don't think it's a bad way to die because you go from feeling relaxed to not feeling anything.'

Over the years snow fell on snow, high up on Tupungato. As it piled up and the pressure increased, so those first, blanketing snows turned to ice. It melded with a glacier that lay where the Lancastrian had crashed. The wreckage and the victims' body parts became entombed. And then, slowly but surely, the glacier began to move down the mountain as glaciers always will. Over the decades that followed fragments of the plane vanished, inched their way down the mountain until they reached the glacier's melt zone, where pieces finally began to emerge on to the moraine. That also explains why the army didn't find anything in 1985 when they first went up to what would eventually be identified as the crash site to recover the bodies of Vierio and Rabal. The wreckage was still locked hard inside the glacier back then. It is likely that 90 per cent of the debris and body parts remain there now, waiting for the moment when they too will be delivered up on to the surface of the moraine.

The investigators released the findings of their investigation in June 2000. They were accepted by Judge Rodríguez in Mendoza and by the Air Accident Investigation Board in Britain. Finally the disappearance of the *Star Dust* – one of the greatest aviation mysteries of all time – had been explained.

By July 2000 the pathologists in Buenos Aires had to admit they had made very little headway with the human remains that had been brought down off Tupungato. They had identified two female hip bones, each belonging to different women. Obviously one belonged to the Stargirl Iris Evans and one to the German émigré Martha Limpert, but they could not say which was which. In addition to the two hip bones they were able to identify seven other separate DNA profiles from among the body fragments provided to them. They believe in total, therefore, that they have the remains of nine of the eleven people who were on board. Beyond that science has proved a disappointment; the DNA was terribly degraded and fragmented and gave the laboratory very little to work with. It has been impossible to identify any of the victims from those fragments, even by magnifying the available DNA many times over. In August 2000 the pathologists informed Judge Rodríguez that the results of the first tests had been 'in-conclusive'. The judge asked them to try again but a year later there was still no answer. It may be that, over the years to come, better preserved pieces of the bodies will emerge out of the glacier from which it will finally be possible to make a positive identification.

The relatives and friends of the victims hold different views as to what should happen with the body parts in the meantime. Lola would like to be able to place the remains of her husband, Casis Said Atalah, in a grave. Others, like Paddy Gooderham, nephew of Jack Gooderham, originally wanted the bodies to be left where they were high up on the mountain, alongside the wreckage which the authorities are not planning to remove. They had spent half a century together, he said. Couldn't they stay there now?

'But I know they can't do that,' he says today, 'because the place where the wreckage was found is bound to become a popular spot for climbers who will try to get there. You can't just have body parts lying about.' Instead there has been the suggestion that all the pieces be cremated together. Then the combined ashes could be distributed among the various families, who could do with them as they wish.

Inevitably it will be for Judge Rodríguez to decide the final resting place of the remains. He will be the one to decide whether the passengers and crew of the *Star Dust* ever make it home.

CHAPTER TWENTY-FIVE

SCIENCE CAN EXPLAIN A LOT OF THINGS, BUT IT IS WEAK IN THE face of myth and legend. Myth and legend have lives of their own which do not need the rich nourishment of fact or evidence; they can survive solely on the power of imagination. The story of the *Star Dust*, the golden plane that vanished in the mountains, has cultivated its own ripe crop. Not least among those legends is the story of Paul Simpson's diplomatic bag. Time and again in the press coverage that followed the discovery of the wreck in January 2000 its contents were described as 'secret' or 'sensitive'. Lying up there, at the foot of the glacier, had to be documents that went to the very heart of South America's volatile political history, reporters announced. In a region with a very long collective memory those papers, if recovered, would surely still be the focus of great intrigue. Anybody who doubts the potency of the diplomatic-bag legend needs only to look back at the way it was used by those 'sources close to' the Argentinian air force when they were trying to justify their pre-emptive strike on the crash site.

Something at least a little sensitive might have been inside the bag, even if it was more canvas sack than sleek attaché case. Relations between Britain and Argentina were very poor at the time. London had far better dealings with Chile, which was where Simpson was heading. Perhaps there genuinely was some delicate matter that the strategists in Whitehall wanted Jack Leche, their man in Santiago, to know.

Lined up on the shelves of the research room at the British government's Public Record Office in Kew, south-west London, is a set of thick volumes, bound in red. It is the index of files created by the Foreign and Commonwealth Office, by whom Paul Simpson was employed. Among the thousands of entries within the volume for 1947 is one that promises an answer. It reads: 'Loss of bags for South America missing on *Star Dust*. Contents list.' After that is a reference code, which is a combination of letters and numbers. That stream of digits must be converted into the PRO's own separate reference code used for those files transferred from their original government department to the archive at Kew. It is a relatively straightforward process which leads, eventually, to another set of heavy bound volumes. These hold the index of all the documents retained by the PRO.

That is assuming that the file you want is one of those that has been retained. The *Star Dust* diplomatic bag file is one of those which, while listed by the Foreign Office, was never transferred to Kew. The swiftest, most enticing conclusion is that the papers were so sensitive, indeed so sensational, they had to be retained for reasons of national security. However, it seems highly unlikely. If a file is being withheld under Britain's draconian secrecy legislation or if it has simply been marked closed for longer than the usual thirty years – as the file on Don Bennett's dismissal was – it says so very clearly in the index. There is no such note attached to the references for this file. It is hardly as if sensitive material is kept back as a matter of course. Recently the PRO released papers detailing the shooting of Irish civilians by British soldiers during Dublin's Easter Uprising of 1916. Documents were also released which revealed that, in the early 1960s, the British government was preparing for the possibility of war with the Soviet Union over its increasing attempts to bring Romania to heel. Is it really likely that the bag Paul Simpson was accompanying contained anything more sensitive than that?

The alternative explanation – that the contents of the bag were so trivial as to be unworthy of the space in the government's crowded archive – makes more sense. According to the archivists at the PRO the file was indeed destroyed at the first possible opportunity in 1947, when it was deemed to be 'unworthy of preservation'. If anybody does ever find the bag on Tupungato they are more likely than not going to be thoroughly disappointed by its contents.

A few days after the *Star Dust* disappeared in 1947 the next BSAA service to Santiago left London. On board was

Captain John Canning of the King's Messenger Corps. Alongside him was another white canvas bag, its neck held closed with a lead seal, as they always were. If the bag contained duplicates of anything that had been lost on the previous flight Canning knew nothing about it.

'Frankly it was a great relief not to know what was inside those bags,' he says today. There was none of that tiresome pressure to keep a secret.

Captain Canning did not know Paul Simpson. Much of the time the King's Messengers were travelling alone so they had little opportunity to meet their colleagues. But he knew full well that his predecessor was lost in the mountains beneath him. 'What I remember most of the trip is the crossing of the Andes,' he says, 'and the crew looking out of the windows in silence in the hope of seeing something below. There was just this terrible sadness about it all.'

He may not be able to shed any light on the mystery of the diplomatic bag but he can help with the legend of the seventy bars of gold: according to Captain Canning, King's Messengers were never called upon to accompany consignments of precious metals about the world. The only thing they ever accompanied was the bag itself and you could not get seventy heavy bars of gold into one of those.

The legend of *Star Dust*'s gold is one of the most potent surrounding the wreck, partly because of the obvious financial value of such a cargo and partly because its existence can only ever be proven by the discovery of the loot up on the mountainside. It is impossible to prove an absence. As long as nobody finds it, to those like José Moiso who want to believe, there is every chance that it might one day turn up.

Gustavo Marón has studied the Argentinian press coverage of the original disappearance in 1947. The popular myth of the *Star Dust* gold lies, he says, in a mixture of assumptions at the time and later true stories that became incorporated into the legend. 'For a start only a wealthy person could afford an airline ticket,' he says. 'Therefore if the passengers were rich it was assumed that they had to be carrying something valuable. And people associate value with gold.' The assumptions about the wealth of the passengers were only reinforced by the duration of the search, which went on for many more days than some people expected (despite the fact that Don Bennett did not feel it had gone on for long enough). Most of those who lived in and around the Andes at the time knew full well that there was no chance of survival up there amid the high winter peaks. So if the army and air force were searching surely it wasn't the people they were looking for. It had to be something else. Then the family of Casis Said Atalah offered thousands of dollars as a reward for any information, only further inflaming the speculation.

In 1972 the myth of the golden plane received a further strong boost when the Mendoza police began hearing stories about five mountain villagers who had been paying for their groceries with gold coins and other valuables. When they were questioned by police they admitted to having ransacked the wreck of an aircraft. At first it was assumed that the wreck they had found was of the *Star Dust*. It turned out they had found the wreck of another plane entirely, a Curtiss C–46 being operated by a North American cargo company, which had disappeared in May

1960. Still, if there was one aircraft rich in gold coin surely there could be another? The legend of the golden plane was, Marón says, able to live on for another few decades.

There is one other explanation for the story of the gold which has nothing to do with either the aircraft or the people who were on board, and everything to do with the mountain upon which it crashed. In 1899 a book called *The Highest Andes* was published by Methuen of London and New York. It was an account of the expedition, mounted two years earlier, during which both Aconcagua and Tupungato were climbed for the first time. In the book Stuart Vines, one of the team who was first to the summit of Tupungato, describes reaching an inn high up in the foothills. After weeks of storms the weather had cleared and it was now crowded with travellers, all preparing to take advantage of the lull to cross the Andes into Chile. Everybody there that night was well aware that the crazy Europeans were not preparing to go across the mountains, but up them. Many of them had advice, Vines wrote, mostly fripperies to do with the weather. There was one contribution described by Vines, however, which is worth repeating in full:

One aged gaucho, with a twinkle in his eye, opined that what we were after was gold. He then held the company's attention by telling us that not far from the top of Tupungato was a lake of great depth – the extinct crater, I mentally decided – around whose shores were immense caves; and that somewhere thereabouts lay a vast quantity of gold, though whether it was on the shores or in the caves or at the bottom of the lake itself, I could not make out. Only one man had ever climbed to it, and on returning . . . had been murdered. His murderers, it seems, had then made an expedition to the mountain, lost their way and with poetic justice perished in the snow. He added that he himself was the only man who knew the secret road to this untold treasure; but I did not understand why he was still a humble shepherd instead of a millionaire in Buenos Aires.

In this story it is the mountain which is golden rather than the plane. Which is more likely? That the *Star Dust* really had seventy gold bars on board when it slammed into the side of Tupungato? Or that an ancient wealth-myth surrounding that part of the Andes somehow became transferred in modern times from the mountains to the aircraft which crashed in them? The alternative explanation, that two different gold myths developed separately but in exactly the same place, demands that the fates deliver up an outrageous coincidence.

There is one last mystery surrounding the *Star Dust*. This, like the legend of the gold, is unlikely ever to be solved to everybody's satisfaction. It concerns Denis Harmer's last seven-letter Morse code message: STENDEC. It was fired off once at the end of a message announcing they were just four minutes away from their Estimated Time of Arrival (ETA). It was sent twice more after that, clear and fast, when the Chilean Morse operator in Santiago queried the word, which he did not recognize as any form of shorthand. After that the radio fell silent. The *Star Dust* was never heard from again.

STENDEC has stood since then as one of the great challenges for Morse code experts everywhere; a bizarre cipher which, if unlocked, could perhaps provide the ultimate answer to what became of the Lancastrian. So potent is the mystery surrounding the word that a corrupted form of it – STENDEK – became the name of a popular science-fiction magazine published in Spain in the 1970s. The magazine never managed to explain the meaning of the word.

Morse code uses combinations of electronic dots and dashes – or 'dits' and 'dahs' as the old hands call them – which, when transmitted by radio, go together to make up letters. It was designed as a clear signal that could cut through the fuzz and clutter that filled the early airwaves far better than the human voice ever could. It is meant to be sharp and precise. In practice, as every user knows, each operator develops their own particular style and some-times, at speed, it can turn into a mere shower of beeps. Most of the suggested solutions to the mystery have depended upon untangling those knots in which Morse often ties itself.

As early as June 1948 a letter appeared in the pages of *Aeroplane* magazine from a wireless operator called Geoffrey Smith who believed he had the answer: the Morse code for STENDEC is just one dot and one short break away from the message ETA LATE, he said. 'This method of signalling a later ETA than the original was, and still is, in use in the RAF,' Smith wrote in 1948. As Harmer was ex-RAF, he concluded, it would make sense that he would use such a shorthand. That's true, though it does not make sense that he would make the same mistake three times or that he would fail to include the number of minutes that he expected to be late. And why would Harmer announce that they were going to be late when he had just announced that they were only four minutes away? ETA LATE offers an answer but not a satisfactory one.

In the autumn of 2000 the documentary the BBC had been shooting up on Tupungato with the Argentinian army's advance expedition was screened, both in Britain and the USA. It included a short sequence on STENDEC. Websites about the *Star Dust* which were set up by the broadcasters to accompany the programme were soon inundated with suggested solutions. Some people simply took STENDEC as an acronym to be broken down, letter by letter. There was 'Stardust Tank Empty No Diesel Expected Crash'. There was 'Santiago Tower Even Navigator Doesn't Exactly Know'. There was the garbled 'Systems To the End Navigation Depends Entirely on Circle'. Carlos Sorini and Luis Estrella also came up with one of these. They favoured 'Severe Turbulence EmergeNcy DEsCent'. Few Morse code experts think it likely, however, that Harmer would have tapped out a convoluted form of initials he could not have expected the operator in Santiago to understand. They also dismiss suggestions that the radio operator was suffering from oxygen deprivation and so garbled the word 'descent' of which STENDEC is an anagram. If he were oxygen deprived why would he come up with the same word spelt exactly the same way three times in a row? In any case while 'descent' and STENDEC are very similar in English they are not at all similar in Morse.

The most convincing explanations come from an analysis of phrases and shorthand used in Morse code at the time. A number of the correspondents started with 'EC', the last two letters of the word. The Morse for 'EC' is exceptionally close to the Morse for 'AR' which has long been used as the sign-off for a Morse code message. Similarly the Morse for the 'ST' at the beginning is exceptionally close to that for 'V' which was used as the call-up sign to start a message. Perhaps it was the Morse code operator in Santiago who took these letters down wrongly. In the middle that would leave just the word 'END' sandwiched between a call-up and a sign-off. Why would Harmer send the word 'END'? Perhaps to inform the airport, which he believed the Lancastrian to be approaching, that he was about to switch to voice communications which could only be used over short distances.

It's a possibility, but no more than that. Unless an ageing textbook turns up listing STENDEC as a recognized Morse shorthand no one will ever know what it meant. While science has managed to tell us a lot about what happened to the *Star Dust* that stormy late afternoon in August of 1947, there are some mysteries it will never be able to solve.

CHAPTER TWENTY-SIX

AT THE TIME DON BENNETT MUST HAVE BELIEVED HIS DISMISSAL from BSAA to be little more than another staging post along the path to greatness. He was not yet forty. He was a leader of men. He had ideas. There was no reason why his future should not be as gilded as his past. It didn't work out like that. While he was never exactly a failure – he had a particular talent for making money – few of his grand schemes ever amounted to much and his increasingly bizarre pronouncements on the state of the nation pushed him to the furthest fringes of British political life. Only in one regard was there any continuity with the past: people still lost their lives on aircraft for which he was responsible.

By chance, 1948 was a good year for a skilled aviator to find himself at a loose end. Within a few weeks of Bennett losing his job the Soviet blockade of Berlin's Allied-controlled zones had begun. Their attempt to challenge the commitment of the British, American and French forces to the former German capital was met by the Berlin Airlift, an effort to keep the city's population supplied. The British government, desperate for air capacity, offered private operators very good rates to get them involved and Bennett accepted the challenge. He was soon based at an airfield near Wunstorf just to the west of Hanover in Germany's British-controlled zone along with two Tudors which had been cleared by the Air Registration Board for carrying freight. He set up a company called Airflight and worked both aircraft to the very limits, flying day and night at enormous profit. Of the 977 return flights to Berlin made by the company from there between June 1948 and May 1949, 250 were flown by Bennett himself.

On one of them he almost killed himself. It was a dismal autumn morning in 1948 with such poor visibility it seemed unlikely the Tudor could fly at all. Eventually, right on the scheduled departure time, the go-ahead was given. Bennett rushed on board and announced to his co-pilot that they were taking off. It was only as they were speeding towards the end of the runway that he realized the tailplane elevators were still locked dead. He couldn't move the control column. Up behind them, in the hold, were thousands of litres of fuel oil destined for Berlin. In front of them, at the very end of the runway, were earth-movers working to extend the landing strip. If he hit the machines the explosion would be massive, instantaneous and fatal. He managed to get the nose up just in time by moving a set of tabs on the tailplane normally only used to control trim. Below him the workmen on the building site threw themselves to the ground to escape the plane's undercarriage as it scraped by overhead.

Now he was up, but he had to get down again. With almost no way of controlling the aircraft the only thing he could do was reduce power. It took four circuits of the airfield to get the landing right. By the time he finally made it down, slamming on to the ground with a heavy thump that practically squeezed the air from the tyres, a vast crowd had gathered. Many of those present were convinced they were witnessing the very last seconds of a legendary aviator's life. Bennett claimed afterwards he had checked that the locks were off. He would never forget to do a thing like that, he said. Clearly, driven by his tendency to gross impatience, he had forgotten. Still, he was alive.

Which is more than could be said for some of Airflight's passengers. In the autumn of 1949 the Air Registration Board finally certified the Tudor to carry passengers once more. The ARB even approved a conversion which meant it could seat up to seventy-eight people, making it the highest-capacity airliner in the world. Bennett's confidence in the great Avro aircraft had been rewarded and he swiftly put the newly converted Tudor to work on charter services. In March 1950 a fully booked Airflight Tudor carrying Welsh Rugby fans from a game in Dublin was flying to an airfield at Llandow just outside Cardiff. According to eyewitnesses the aircraft's nose went up just as it was making the final approach. Then it dived into a field and exploded. Two people, who had been seated in the tail, escaped unhurt. Another eighty were killed. It was the worst death toll in civil aviation history up to that point.

Despite an official enquiry, the crash was never explained.

Bennett withdrew from carrying passengers soon after that. He didn't have the stomach for it any more. For a few months he carried on flying freight, but in the early 1950s he sold the company. There were grand projects in the years that followed, but something always went wrong. Invariably he claimed it was the fault of grossly anti-competitive action by government officials who were set on suffocating business. A plan to introduce flying boats on to the South American routes BOAC had abandoned in the mid-1950s was, he said, destroyed by government dithering. By the time Whitehall gave their approval Bennett's financial backers had pulled out and taken their money elsewhere. An attempt to market a new private plane in Britain was ruined because the government had invested millions of pounds in the development of a direct competitor. His ambitions to expand a small airport outside London called Blackbushe, which he owned, were thwarted, he said, because the local parish council would not sell him the extra land he needed to make it a viable concern. Officials were always getting in the way. As Bennett saw it they had always got in his way; surely they weren't going to stop now?

As well as these very public battles with civil servants, there was one that Bennett fought rather more quietly. In the early 1950s the Civil Aviation Ministry changed the qualifying standards for the renewal of aircraft navigators' licences. Previously an applicant had to show they had served as a navigator for a minimum of just six hours during the previous year. In 1953 that limit was raised by law to twenty hours. Bennett didn't have enough time on his logbook. Don Bennett, author of the standard text on aircraft navigation, was refused a navigator's licence. He wrote a furious letter to the ministry. 'I have, as you know, more navigation experience than most people in this world,' he wrote. 'And internationally I'm accepted as one of the leading practical navigators.'

A month later he wrote again: 'When one has learnt to swim,' he said, 'one does not forget. Similarly the handling of an aeroplane or the navigation thereof are not things one forgets.' Within weeks the ministry caved in and gave him his licence. For the next few years whenever it became time to renew, Bennett simply scribbled across the bottom of his application form: 'Request renewal on the basis of general experience.' And the official did as he was told.

In 1956, however, the civil servant concerned decided that it was an issue for the aviation minister. Bennett's navigator's licence could easily have become a major political problem, if the press ever got wind of it.

'We are constantly having trouble with AVM Bennett who has a natural instinct to be lawless,' the official wrote. 'Recently we had under consideration whether to prosecute him for not complying with the prescribed procedure on a flight between Denham and Manchester.'

'The minister accepts that it seems a bit much to be rough on the former leader of the Pathfinders,' a secretary said, on the minister's behalf. 'But there can be no exceptions.' Bennett – the greatest navigator of his age – again lost his navigator's licence. It was a secret he kept even from his closest family members.

It may be that it was this experience which motivated his increasingly anti-government political pronouncements, which started at around the same time. In the introduction to his memoir, *Pathfinder*, first published in 1958, he once again accused the British government of behaving like the Nazi party, just as he had done at a Liberal Party rally in May of 1947. At meetings across the country he now argued furiously for Britain to keep out of the European Economic Community. The EEC, he said, was a hotbed of bureaucracy. What's more it was run by nations who were often Britain's enemies or 'supporters of our enemies'. He also helped establish and run a number of anti-European organizations.

Eventually he appeared to form a distinctly unholy alliance with representatives of Britain's racist right. In 1971 he took part in a ceremony at London's Cenotaph honouring the dead of Rhodesia and South Africa – already pariah states because of their apartheid policies – which had been organized by the avowedly racist National Front party. Likewise, he campaigned against the government's decision to allow into the country Asians who had been expelled from Uganda by the dictator Idi Amin. In September 1972 Bennett addressed a rally against the Ugandan Asians at London's Smithfield meat market, again attended by supporters of the NF. Standing before a small crowd, many of them waving banners bearing the legend 'Britain for the British', he called upon the government to withdraw any British passports that had already been distributed to Asians.

He did once try to defend himself against accusations

that he was a racist. He was not the one who had joined the NF, he said. They had joined him. 'This is the National Front technique,' he told an interviewer. 'They find out there is a rally somewhere, or even a sporting event, and they go along and tag on.' On one occasion he issued a writ against the Young Socialists when they claimed in one of their publications that he was a member of a fascist organization. After all it would be distinctly odd if a man whose reputation was built upon his contribution to a war against the forces of Nazism were himself to share their ideology. On another occasion, however, he was asked by a journalist to condemn the NF's brand of politics. 'So far as I know,' he replied tartly, 'the National Front are British and perfectly respectable.' Not long afterwards he was involved in the foundation of an organization calling itself the Independent Democratic Movement. It advocated a programme of voluntary repatriation of immigrants.

While increasingly he was being ostracized by the British establishment his men still held him in high regard, if not for his politics then certainly for his skills as a flier. At the regular reunions of those who had flown under his command with the Pathfinders and BSAA, Bennett and his wife Ly were always the guests of honour. He in turn could look proudly upon those whom he had employed. Many of them had gone on to enjoy hugely successful careers in civil aviation. Cliff Alabaster, second in command aboard BSAA's inaugural service out of Heathrow on 1 January 1946, transferred to BOAC and stayed with them right into the jet age. For the first few years he remained on the Santiago route, piloting propeller-driven Argonauts which continued to hop their way down through Spain, Africa and Brazil to Buenos Aires. In 1954 BOAC suspended services to South America when they needed the aircraft for other routes; the Comet, an early jet airliner, had been withdrawn due to concerns over its safety record and they needed the Argonauts to pick up the slack. Alabaster moved on to flying services to the four corners of the globe. In time he became the first pilot to take a civil jet into both Auckland and Tokyo. He retired in 1973 but civil aviation is still in the family: one of his sons is now an airline pilot.

Archie Jackson, who joined BSAA after that perfunctory meeting with the chief executive at the Plaza Hotel in Buenos Aires in 1946, also stayed with BOAC. He ended his career aboard Vickers VC–10s. Sometimes he was able to get himself on to his beloved South American routes, working his way back down to Santiago where he had been born and still had family. More often, like Alabaster, he was piloting services to North America or Africa or Asia. He retired in 1977. By then the company was called British Airways, its name today.

For many years the commercial route to South America, which Don Bennett had pioneered, changed very little. Right into the 1970s the services continued to hop their way down through Europe and Africa before making for Argentina and Chile. Sometimes Madrid was substituted for Lisbon; usually the airliners went into Recife in Brazil, rather than Natal. But the concept of the multi-stage journey, inaugurated in 1946, remained exactly the same, even if the airline operating the service didn't. The South

American route became something of a poor relation, dropped by BOAC then picked up again by British United Airways or British Caledonian (both of which were eventually merged into British Airways) only to be dropped once more. It wasn't until the 1970s, with the introduction of the first 747s, that it was possible to do anything approaching a non-stop journey from Britain to South America.

With the outbreak of the Falklands/Malvinas War in 1982 all flights to Argentina from Britain were suspended. They resumed again in 1990, with a British Airways service to Buenos Aires and Santiago via Rio. In the mid-1990s the 747s finally began flying to Buenos Aires non-stop before taking off again for what was the remaining leg of that original route across the high Andes to Santiago, created almost half a century before by BSAA. In August 2000, however, British Airways scrapped the service. They handed the trans-Andean stretch over to their partner-airline Lan Chile. It made little sense keeping British pilots trained up for what is, even today, an interesting aviation challenge. British Airways, the company directly descended from BSAA, can no longer see a good commercial reason to cross the Andes, the mountains which, half a century ago, swallowed up a plane called *Star Dust*, its captain Reginald Cook, and ten others.

With what looked like military precision Don Bennett died on his birthday, 14 September, in 1986. He was 76 years old. His obituary in *The Times* described him as 'an outstanding figure in British civil and military aviation, whose forceful personality earned him enemies as well as friends'. There was no doubting his talent, it said. The man had done just about everything there was to do in the field of aviation by the end of the war: he had secured the seaplane record; he had conquered the north Atlantic; he had commanded the Pathfinders. But, it added, 'it would be charitable to describe his political attitudes as ill-thought-out and immature'.

That was the tragedy of Don Bennett: he believed he was owed something for the service he had given during the war. He felt he should have been taken seriously; that he should have been treated like the great leader he once had been. But the post-war world had refused to fall into line with his intricate designs for it and that infuriated him beyond words. He ended his life a thoroughly disappointed man.

CHAPTER TWENTY-SEVEN

GEORGE CHECKLIN NEVER FORGOT THE PROMISE HE MADE TO his mother, Mary, by the heavy wooden fireplace at her home in West Bridgford. She would not rest easy until she knew what had happened to Donald. His brother would simply have to make the journeys that she could not. He would have to travel to the Andes. There was no other way.

George was the right man for the job. In the late summer of 1948, during a break from postgraduate studies at Oxford University, he mounted a solo expedition to Iceland's Ódádahraun lava desert. He wanted to collect geological specimens from one of the youngest and roughest stretches of rock on the planet, a lonely place where people are as rare as palm trees. A photograph taken just before he departed shows a dark-browed young man with a flop of black hair, in canvas trousers and jacket. Under his arm is a rolled-up map. He looks as though he is preparing to yomp through the Lake District rather than one of the most inhospitable pieces of wilderness on earth.

Perhaps that's what he thought the Ódádahraun desert would be like, because he was certainly underprepared. Within a few days he was completely lost amid the brittle, snow-swept lava fields. His compass had revolted against the bizarre magnetic fields thrown out by the mountains and become less a source of direction than distraction. Soon after that he realized he had neither enough food nor the right equipment to cope with the conditions. For over a week George wandered alone across 360 square miles of Iceland's undersurveyed hinterland, surviving on cocoa made with melted snow and the few chunks of chocolate he could allow himself each day. Eventually he stumbled across a shepherd tending his flock, who fed him and gave him shelter.

When George's story reached Reykjavik the press dubbed him 'the mad Englishman'. He had survived a journey that not even an Icelandic native would attempt, and with so little equipment. He returned to England in October 1948, by working his passage as a galley boy aboard an oil tanker, and made headlines once more. 'I think the people there thought I was a bit mad,' he told a reporter from the *Nottinghamshire Evening News* on his arrival home. But he liked Iceland, he said. The people were pleasant and he might one day go back.

By comparison the two trips he made to the Andes during the 1950s to search for the truth about his brother must have been relatively straightforward. He funded his journeys from money made on a big uranium find in northern Canada, and spent almost two years travelling through the remotest villages high up in the mountains closest to where the *Star Dust* had last been heard from. Wherever he went he asked questions, but nobody he met knew anything about the plane he was looking for. There was only one lead: he came across a Native American wearing what he later described as a British watch. The same man also had a compass which, George swore, was RAF issue. He questioned the man endlessly, begged him to say where he had found both items, but the man refused to tell him anything.

George had heard the rumours about the gold. He wondered whether the Argentinian was keeping quiet because he really had found the wreck but didn't want to let on in case the authorities came looking for the bullion. Then again, George said, there were a lot of plane crashes in the Andes. It happened all the time. Maybe the watch and the compass had come from a different aircraft. That was always possible. It left him no nearer to finding out what had happened to his brother.

He didn't return to the Andes but his hunger to solve the mystery remained undiminished, even with the death of Mary Checklin in 1959. Now George was alone; he was the very last of his family. In the 1960s he made his home in Calgary, Alberta, a Canadian city at the heart of the oil and mineral industry, where he worked for Scurry-Rainbow Oil and Gas. There he met a widowed secretary called Melva Day who had three daughters, and he fell for her. He called her 'Sunny' and eventually asked her to marry him but, while Melva was very fond of George, she didn't love him. Not in that way. Eventually she married somebody else instead.

Still, Melva and George remained firm and close friends and he became an unofficial member of her large extended prairie family. The prairies were a place where you could reinvent yourself, become whoever you wanted to be, and George liked that about them. Similarly, the large, boisterous family gave him somewhere to belong, which was something he was lacking. He was always there around the crowded table at Christmas and Easter, or to celebrate birthdays and weddings, revelling in the complex mix of intellectuals and farmers, of young and old. Their combined interests were as varied as his own.

The brood was headed by Melva's father, a Norwegian immigrant called Ingeman Erickson who had lived a hard life farming his way across Canada. He and George understood each other and after the death of Ingeman's wife they spent a lot of time together just talking, always talking. At other times George entertained the small children with magic tricks, pulling coins from behind soft ears, or he gave the older kids books to read that he thought they might like. Now that he was certain he would never have children of his own, he quietly spread a little of his cash about, making anonymous donations to help some of the younger ones with college fees or simply to get them through a tight spot.

One night over the dinner table, when George wasn't there, Melva told her three growing daughters, Debbie, Patti and Anita, the story of his lost brother. A little later, when Patti was grieving over a death in the family, she talked to George about Donald. 'I asked him where he thought people go when they die,' Patti says today. 'And he suggested things that I could read, because he had researched all of the religions.' Towards the end of his life he even joined two churches, despite a lifelong uncertainty about the value of one religion over another. These were clearly churches for a man in pursuit of something. One was called the Centre for Positive Living; the other was the Calgary First Spiritualist Church. At the same time he became intrigued by the idea of UFOs and read enormous amounts on the subject. All of it, Patti says, was George's attempt to make sense of his lost brother. He always said there was nothing odd about the efforts he was making. Donald would have done the same for him if George had been the one who was lost. It was that sort of relationship.

'George was searching,' she says. 'Always searching. He said that he deeply regretted losing contact with his family after the death of an aunt and that he wanted to get back in touch with them. And eventually he did. He found two cousins in Vancouver, but they were unresponsive and nothing came of it.'

The question of Donald was there as a backbeat to everything he did. He was obsessed by the story of the King's Messenger: just what had he been carrying? Long before the crash investigators advanced the avalanche theory he came up with it as an explanation for why the wreck had never been found. And he nagged endlessly at the STENDEC question. 'The STENDEC thing really bugged him because he could never pin it down despite the fact that he was so well educated,' Patti says. 'This was a man who could recite huge amounts of poetry. He had studied philosophy. He was an expert in flora and fauna. But he could never answer that question. He considered the possibility of it being a word in another language. He wondered whether it had been another passenger who had sent the message.' But, as with everything else, nothing came of it.

In the late 1970s George developed health problems and in November 1978 he suffered a massive heart attack. For two days he lay in the intensive-care unit at Calgary's Holy Cross Hospital. The medical staff prepared the family of which he had become such a part for the worst. He might not make it, they said, but eventually his condition appeared to stabilize. The day before he was due to be moved to a standard ward Patti was told she could talk to him. Before the heart attack, when he knew he was ailing, George had asked her to be the executor of his will. She was the logical person for him to share his thoughts with now. It soon became clear to her that there was one thought preying on his mind more than any other.

'He was very concerned that if they found Donald's body after he was gone there would be nobody left to say "I know who he is",' Patti says.

'There will be nobody to say he belongs in Nottingham,' George had told her. 'That he was a war hero, that he was a wonderful adventurer, that he was a brilliant man.'

Patti made a promise to George just as he had made a promise to his mother, Mary: she would be the keeper of his memories. She would speak up for Donald. She would make sure that people knew who Donald Checklin was.

George Checklin died in hospital on 26 November 1978. He was fifty-seven years old.

Patti was preparing breakfast on the morning of 26 January 2000 when her husband, Dave, spotted the news story in the *Calgary Herald*. 'Patti, come and read this,' he shouted. 'I think they've found George's brother's plane.'

She read the story. Only a few weeks before they had been talking about George and Donald. Her family had given Patti a computer for Christmas. She had been using it to put together all the material she had about her extended family into one album so she could pass it on to her own daughter. Now she retrieved the papers and the photographs and began sifting through them: the original crash report and the letters from Mary Checklin on fragile onion-skin paper and those photographs of the two handsome brothers as young men, both with their unruly hair.

'I concluded that if George were alive he'd have called the newspaper,' Patti says. 'He'd have got whatever details he could from the journalist and then hopped on the first flight to Buenos Aires to head up a recovery team. I was forgetting he would be in his seventies.'

She talked it over with Dave. They agreed that she should call the *Herald* to ask that, as the executor of George's will, she be kept in touch with any developments. They sent round a journalist and the next day it was *her* picture that appeared on the front page of the newspaper. It wasn't what she had intended at all. She wanted them to tell George and Donald's story.

At least she would be able to make amends with the family album she was compiling, now that she could conclude the story. George, she wrote, 'was a true gentleman.

He was kind, generous and caring . . . He was a wonderful friend who listened but didn't judge.'

She added, 'I promised him that our family would keep their memories and that we would speak for him. I had a lot of responsibilities to fulfil to execute George's wishes in his will. This album is my final obligation. I hope to be able to add something more about Donald's final resting place.' She had kept the story of the Checklin family alive. She had kept her promise.

CHAPTER TWENTY-EIGHT

GEORGE CHECKLIN'S STORY ABOUT THE NATIVE AMERICAN with the heavy British watch on his wrist is one of a number about the *Star Dust* that have surfaced over the years. Each one raises the possibility that the wreck was found a long time before Alejo Moiso and Sergeant Cardozo finally located it up on Tupungato in January 2000. Each time, however, the 'confirmed' sightings turned out to be just rumours or fragments of fact that had become heavily embroidered in the telling. Late in life Don Bennett himself informed one aviation historian that George Checklin had not just spoken to the man wearing the watch, he had got answers too. Apparently the Native American said he found it dangling from the wrist of a skeleton sprawled by the wreck of an aircraft. Later, Bennett claimed, the man even led a search party to the site where the fragments of the *Star Dust* were finally identified. If so, the search party kept it very quiet because there is no record anywhere of either such an expedition or such a find, apart from Bennett's word on it.

After the first reports of the plane's discovery late in 1947, which the Civil Aviation Ministry had dismissed as pure unsubstantiated rumour in letters to relatives of the victims, the next apparent sighting came in December 1955. 'Lost plane found – after 8 years', announced the *News Chronicle* in Britain. 'Eight years after its disappearance in the Andes with 11 people on board,' the short news story announced, 'the wreckage of a British airliner has been found, BOAC said last night.' Other press reports claimed a Chilean expedition was already on the way to the scene, which the Chilean government swiftly denied. No official Chilean expedition was going anywhere unless there was solid information.

The news sent the British Foreign Office into a flurry of activity. Officials quickly wired their embassy in Santiago and demanded to know who the source was. It came, the embassy replied, from a Mr Reid, BOAC's representative in Chile. 'Reid . . . states that he was approached in strict confidence by the legal representative of the original informant whom he has not been able to see in person,' Mr Hankey of the British embassy wired back to London. '[The] informant has so far not revealed any details or substantive evidence, apparently in the hope of obtaining promise of recompense.' The reward from Casis Said Atalah's family was, after all, still outstanding.

Within days letters arrived at the Civil Aviation Ministry from Aubrey Harmer, brother of Denis, and Paddy

Gooderham, brother of Jack. Both demanded to know what the British government intended to do about the reports, as did BOAC, which had received similar letters. The chief inspector of accidents wrote emollient letters to the relatives. The stories were just rumours, he said, and had not been substantiated. We thank you for your interest. We will keep in touch. Yours faithfully.

The problem, the chief inspector explained to his colleagues, was that nobody even knew whether the *Star Dust* really had crashed in Chile. It disappeared over border country and could quite easily be lying on Argentinian soil; Argentina would then be responsible for any expedition. As one British government official put it at the time, in a confidential memo for internal consumption only, 'Our interest is indeed only the negative and indirect one that we should not wish the Chilean Government to be pressed to carry out a search if the result is a bill for the expenditure.' What's more, added the chief inspector in another memo, it was hardly as if they were going to learn anything of technical value from the wreck after so much time. Far better, then, for everybody to keep their heads down and do nothing.

It didn't stop reports about the plane from surfacing. In January 1958 the *Star* newspaper announced that the wreck had been located in the Andes by a German climber. No serious attempt was made to follow up the report. Two years later, in May 1960, there was yet another. An Argentinian transport aircraft had gone missing on a flight from Buenos Aires to Panama. Patrols searching for it had sighted wreckage at around 15,000 feet up the Overo volcano in the Andes. According to the patrols the wreckage was thought to belong not to the missing transport plane but to *Star Dust*. The chief inspector of accidents wired the British air attaché in Lima, Peru, for more information. He replied in August. 'From the information in our possession,' he wrote, 'it is deduced that the remains of the aircraft found do not correspond to the English aircraft Lancastrian G–AGWH *Star Dust*.' It was just some other aircraft that had fallen foul of the sudden turbulence in the Andes.

The most intriguing story emerged a full ten years later. In October and November 1970 Peter Young's journalist niece, Stacy Marking, was in Santiago to interview the newly elected Chilean president, Salvador Allende, for her newspaper. 'While I was there reports appeared in the Chilean press saying that a glacier on Tupungato had melted back up the mountain,' she says today, 'and that an aircraft fuselage had been sighted.' There were even reports that bodies had been found. 'I thought I owed it to my uncle to make sure he got a decent burial,' Stacy says. But she had no way of mounting an expedition of her own and by the time she had moved over the Andes to Argentina early in 1971 nobody knew anything about the supposed sighting. She assumed that whatever was up there had been covered up again by the deep Andean snows.

For all the grand rumours it seemed there was no tangible evidence that anybody else had found the wreckage of the *Star Dust* before Alejo Moiso and Sergeant Cardozo in January 2000 – or, to give first credit where credit is due, Pablo Reguera and Fernando Garmendia in

January 1998. At least that seemed to be the case until the day in February 2000 when the Argentinian air force beat their army colleagues to the wreckage by landing two helicopters alongside it. In one sequence of the video shot that day on the mountainside, Major Luis Estrella of the AAIB squats down on to his haunches. He picks up a strip of frayed leather which turns out to be a man's wallet. Methodically he rips the leather to pieces, allowing fragments to fall gently to the ground as he turns it inside out. It is as if he is searching for something. When the sequence appeared on the television news in Mendoza that evening it infuriated José Moiso.

'We are always respectful of any remains or wreckage that we find at crash sites,' he said later with undisguised contempt. 'But the air-force man? He just stood there tearing the wallet apart.' To José it was proof of what a freak show the whole expedition had become.

But Major Estrella wasn't particularly interested in the wallet, only its contents. Despite the years that had passed up on Tupungato even paper documents had managed to survive the passage of time, as Alejo Moiso himself found when he first discovered the wreckage. The pieces of paper were incredibly fragile and tended to disintegrate into nothing more than dust the moment they were touched but, preserved by the cold and low levels of oxygen up this high, they had survived all the same.

As the leather now falls apart in his hands Major Estrella finally offers up a commentary to the camera. 'Here we can see a wallet,' he says. 'Apparently it has no documents, no identification. There's only the leather of the wallet. No personal objects.' Then he looks up and says: 'Somebody has been here before us. No doubt about it.' He drops the tattered leather back on to a rock and moves on to the next piece of wreckage. He doesn't think to take the empty bill fold with him. The wallet has lain in one place or another on this mountainside for over half a century. It might as well stay here now.

BIBLIOGRAPHY

Barnes, C. H. (1989) *Shorts Aircraft Since 1900*, Putnam Aeronautical Books.

Bennett, D. (1958) *Pathfinder*, Fredrick Muller Ltd.

Bramson, A. (1985) *Master Airman: a biography of Air Vice Marshal Donald Bennett*, Airlife Publishing Ltd.

Brown, D. (1974) 'British South American Airways: some recollections', *Air Pictorial*, November and December.

Burge, C. G. (ed.) (1935) *Encyclopaedia of Aviation*, Sir Isaac Pitman & Sons Ltd.

Davies, R. E. G. (1964) *A History of the World's Airlines*, Oxford University Press.

Fitzgerald, E. (ed.) (1899) *The Highest Andes: a record of the first ascent of Aconcagua and Tupungato in Argentina and the exploration of the surrounding valleys*, Methuen.

Hennessy, A. & King, J. (eds) (1992) *The Land that England Lost: Argentina and Britain, a special relationship*, British Academic Press. (Especially: Howells, G., 'The British press and the Peróns', for quotation from *The Economist* on page 80; Jones, C. A., 'British capital in Argentine history: structure, rhetoric and change'; and Macdonald, C., 'End of Empire: the decline of the Anglo-Argentine connection 1918–51'.)

Hoare, R. (1956) *Wings over the Atlantic*, Phoenix House Ltd.

Hyde, H. M. (1968) *Strong for Service: a biography of Lord Nathan of Churt*, W. H. Allen.

Jackson, A. S. (1991) *Pathfinder Bennett, Airman Extraordinary*, Terence Dalton Ltd.

Jackson, A. S. (1997) *Can Anyone see Bermuda?: memories of an airline pilot (1941–1976)*, Cirrus Associates.

Jarrett, P. (2000) 'Captain Cook's last voyage', *Aeroplane Monthly*, April.

McCullough, A. (1997) 'Next week, air! The story of the Mayo Composite', *Airpower*, July.

Nyman, M. (1998) 'Bangers to Buenos Aires, the short – and rather shocking – history of BSAA, 1946–49', *Aeroplane Monthly*, July.

Stroud, J. (1992) 'Post-war propliners', *Aeroplane Monthly*, June.

ACKNOWLEDGEMENTS

HALF A CENTURY BACK IN TIME IS A LONG WAY TO TRAVEL AND I was fortunate to have many guides to show me the way. I am indebted to the biographies of Air Vice-Marshal Don Bennett by Alan Bramson and Archie Jackson, both of which drew upon Bennett's own memoir (see bibliography). All three books provided invaluable detail on his early life and career described in chapters two and four of this book. Torix Bennett, Donald's son, helped me to gain an understanding of his complex father.

Many former staff of British South American Airways gave willingly of both their time and memories. I extend my thanks to the pilots: Cliff Alabaster, Archie Jackson, Lincoln Lee, Donald Mackintosh (who also gave me access to his, as yet unpublished, memoir of the BSAA days) and Jeff Rees. Captain Frank Taylor provided the photograph of the *Star Dust*. Then there are the Stargirls: Mary

Cunningham née Guthrie, Pat Gummer, Sylvia Haynes, Zoë Jenner and Jean Storey neé Fowler. Keith Hayward, a former BSAA employee who now helps oversee the British Airways archive which covers the BSAA days, was a constant source of contact numbers, documents and detail on the airline.

It is entirely possible that, out of loyalty to the company and the friends who died working for it, a number of these former BSAA employees will be unhappy with the full story of the airline told in this book. While I acknowledge their great help I am in no way claiming their endorsement. Nevertheless, I am very grateful to them all.

I would also like to thank: Sir Peter Masefield, who gave me invaluable insights into the workings of the Civil Aviation Ministry and its relationship with Bennett during his tenure there in the 1940s; Lucinda Brown and the staff of the Public Record Office in Kew, who helped me to obtain hundreds of pages of previously unseen documents about both the *Star Dust* and BSAA; Jim Woodhead and John Sheard at the Department of the Environment, Transport and the Regions, who were remarkably speedy in granting me early access to the file on Bennett's dismissal which was not due to be opened until 2024; Brian Riddle, chief librarian of the Royal Aeronautical Society; Katie Parker of the Foreign and Commonwealth Office press office; Andres Federman, Maria Elisa Costa and Hugh Elliott of the British embassy in Buenos Aires; the staff of the British Airways press office; Captain Jim Fomes of British Airways.

I am particularly grateful to all the friends and relatives

of those who died aboard the *Star Dust*, who shared with me correspondence, photographs and sometimes very painful memories. First the passengers: in Santiago, Chile, Casis Said Atalah's widow Lola Samur Samur and their son Nazir Atalah Samur; also in Santiago, Martha Limpert's grandson Rudolpho Limpert; in Western Canada, Jack Gooderham's nephew Paddy Gooderham (and Paddy's wife June); in Pennsylvania, USA, Harald Pagh's niece Stella Gabudza; in Britain, Paul Simpson's niece Christine Reese; also in Britain, Peter Young's nieces Mary Lowerson and Stacy Marking.

The crew, all in Britain: Reginald Cook's brother-in-law John Parker; Hilton Cook's nephew Christopher Cook; Denis Harmer's sister Olive Coombs and her son Simon Coombs; Donald Checklin's cousin Margaret Coalwood and Checklin's friend Nina Brauer-Walton. Finally, in Calgary, Canada, George Checklin's friend Patti Holmes.

Jonathan Renouf of BBC television's *Horizon* programme was extraordinarily generous with the contacts that he, and his colleagues Eugenie Samuels and Alicky Lockhart, had gathered for their programme on the *Star Dust*. They led me to a number of those relatives and friends that I had not already tracked down.

In Mendoza, Argentina, I would like to thank: José and Alejo Moiso and their friend Facundo Brown; Gustavo Marón; Atilio Baldini, who gave me a piece of *Star Dust* wreckage; Pablo Reguera; Colonel Mario Luis Chretien of the Argentinian army's Eighth Mountain Brigade; Lieutenant Colonel Ricardo Bustos of the Eleventh Mountain Regiment; Major Gonzalo Javier de la Rue of the Eleventh Mountain Regiment; Sergeant Armando Cardozo of the Eleventh Mountain Regiment; Carlos Sorini of the Argentinian Air Accident Investigation Board; Major Luis Estrella, also of the AAIB; Carlos Bauzá; Judge Alfredo Rodríguez.

Nicolás García, then of *Los Andes* newspaper, not only described the journalists' expedition on Tupungato, he also helped me find my way about Mendoza, helped with fact-checking in the later stages and supplied me with a stream of exceptionally patient interpreters. They are: Ileana Spano, Alison Llaver and Claudia Weisz. Rosamund Hitchcock of R & R Teamwork in London put me in touch with José Asensio of Santa Julia Wines in Mendoza, who made sure I was suitably accommodated. In Santiago Jonathan Franklin of the *Guardian* and *Observer* newspapers helped me find my way about the city and found me my resilient interpreter, Rossana Santis.

Klaus Dobbs of Royal Holloway, University of London gave me advice on Anglo-Argentinian relations in the relevant period. Margaret Ecclestone of the Alpine Club library helped me find the unfindable. The research staff of the *Guardian* and *Observer* newspapers library dug out rare cuttings for me. Colonel John Kimmins, historian of the King's Messenger Corps, shared with me his research. Captain John Canning, formerly of the King's Messenger Corps, shared with me his recollections. My mother, Claire Rayner, gave advice on matters medical. My father, Des Rayner, gave advice on the fashions of the 1940s. The editor of the *Observer*, Roger Alton, and its managing editor, John Duncan, were exceptionally patient with me when I disappeared from the office for three months to write this book.

As well as giving of his time Cliff Alabaster read the manuscript for technical errors. All mistakes remain my own, however. At my British publishers, Transworld, my first editor, Jo Goldsworthy, showed the initial enthusiasm needed to make a project like this a reality; she passed on the baton to my current editor, the equally fine, astute and enthusiastic Sarah Westcott. My agent, Pat Kavanagh at PFD, made exactly the right sort of encouraging noises.

Finally, my wife, Pat Gordon Smith, read every page as it was written, made wise and incisive suggestions and was always ready with a full glass of wine when my spirits flagged. As with everything in my life I simply couldn't have done it without her.

In memory of those who
died aboard the

STAR DUST

on

2 August 1947

Passengers
Casis Said Atalah
Jack Gooderham
Martha Limpert
Harald Pagh
Paul Simpson
Peter Young

Crew
Donald Checklin
Hilton Cook
Reginald Cook
Iris Evans
Denis Harmer